Veil of Phantom Whispers

Unveiling the Mysteries of the Invisible World

Louise Snider

Chapter 1: The Enigma of Phantom Whispers

The Origin of Phantom Whispers

Phantom whispers, those elusive murmurs that seem to echo from the depths of the unseen, have long fascinated and perplexed humanity. These whispers, often described as faint voices or sounds with no discernible source, have been woven into the fabric of human experience since ancient times. Their origin, shrouded in mystery, has led to a multitude of interpretations and theories that span cultural, spiritual, and psychological dimensions.

From the earliest days of human consciousness, whispers were often attributed to the presence of spirits or otherworldly beings. In many ancient cultures, these whispers were seen as messages from the divine or the deceased, offering guidance, warnings, or insights. The belief that the spirits of ancestors or gods communicated through whispers was widespread, and rituals were developed to interpret and respond to these ethereal messages. Shamans, priests, and spiritual leaders acted as intermediaries, using their perceived connection to the spiritual realm to decipher the whispers' meanings.

As civilizations evolved, the notion of phantom whispers continued to captivate the human imagination. In ancient Greece, the oracles were believed to receive messages from the gods, which were sometimes perceived as whispers carried on the wind. These whispers were thought to provide divine guidance, influencing decisions in matters of state and personal dilemmas alike. Similarly, in the Norse sagas, whispers were often associated with the presence of the Norns, the mythical beings who controlled fate, their voices offering glimpses into the future.

The idea of whispers as a bridge between the human and the supernatural persisted into the Middle Ages, where they were frequently linked to the realm of the occult. In this period, whispers were often associated with witchcraft and sorcery, believed to be the voices of spirits summoned by practitioners of the dark arts. The fear and fascination with these whispers led to the infamous witch hunts, as society grappled with the perceived threat of malevolent forces communicating through unseen channels.

In addition to spiritual interpretations, phantom whispers have been deeply embedded in cultural folklore. Stories of haunted locations where whispers echo through the halls, or tales of mysterious voices heard in the wilderness, abound in the folklore of diverse cultures. These stories often serve to explain the unexplainable, providing a narrative framework for experiences that defy logical explanation. In some cultures, whispers are believed to be the voices of nature spirits or elementals, entities that inhabit the natural world and communicate with humans in subtle ways.

The psychological dimension of phantom whispers offers yet another layer of complexity to their origin. Modern psychology suggests that whispers may be a manifestation of the subconscious mind, a phenomenon where repressed thoughts, emotions, or memories surface in auditory form. This perspective posits that whispers arise from the depths of the psyche, giving voice to the internal conflicts and desires that remain hidden from conscious awareness. In this view, whispers become a tool for self-exploration, offering insights into the inner workings of the mind.

In literature and art, phantom whispers have been employed as a powerful narrative device, symbolizing the inner voice or conscience of a character. Authors and artists have used whispers to convey a sense of unease or foreboding, to illustrate the struggle between opposing forces within an individual, or to emphasize the thin boundary between reality and imagination. The ambiguity of whispers allows for a rich tapestry of interpretation, inviting audiences to explore themes of perception, belief, and the unknown.

Real-life accounts of phantom whispers add yet another dimension to their enigmatic nature. Many individuals report experiences of hearing whispers without any apparent source, often in moments of solitude or heightened emotion. These experiences can range from comforting to unsettling, and individuals often struggle to explain them using conventional logic. While skeptics may attribute these occurrences to auditory hallucinations or environmental factors, others believe they represent genuine interactions with the unseen world.

In the quest to understand phantom whispers, scientific inquiry has sought to demystify their origin. Researchers have explored the possibility of auditory phenomena caused by environmental factors, such as wind patterns, acoustics, or electromagnetic fields. Studies in the field of neuropsychology have examined the brain's role in processing auditory information, offering insights into how the mind can create the perception of whispers in the absence of external stimuli.

Despite these efforts, the origin of phantom whispers remains an open question, a tantalizing mystery that continues to elude definitive explanation. The whispers serve as a reminder of the vast unknown that lies beyond the boundaries of human understanding, inviting curiosity and speculation about the nature of reality and the limits of perception. They challenge us to consider the possibility of dimensions beyond the visible, where whispers carry the secrets of the universe.

Cultural Interpretations and Folklore

Throughout history, whispers have transcended boundaries, bridging cultural divides and weaving themselves into the tapestry of folklore across the globe. Each culture, with its unique tapestry of beliefs and traditions, offers its own interpretation of these mysterious murmurs. This rich diversity of interpretations has given rise to a multitude of stories, each reflecting the values, fears, and hopes of the society from which it originates.

In the labyrinth of cultural interpretations, whispers are often perceived as omens or harbingers of change. In some Native American traditions, for instance, whispers are seen as the voices of ancestors imparting wisdom or warnings to the living. These whispers guide individuals on their spiritual journeys, serving as a compass in the intricate dance between the physical and spiritual worlds. The whispers are believed to offer insights into the interconnectedness of all life, urging individuals to live in harmony with nature and the universe.

In the Celtic tradition, whispers are often associated with the Sidhe, the fairy folk who inhabit the hidden realms of the Earth. These ethereal beings are said to communicate through whispers, their voices carrying messages that reveal the secrets of the natural world. The whispers of the Sidhe are believed to hold the power to enchant or bewilder, drawing the listener into a realm where the ordinary rules of time and space dissolve. The tales of the Sidhe reflect a deep reverence for nature, emphasizing the delicate balance between humanity and the unseen forces that shape the world.

Similarly, in Japanese folklore, whispers are linked to the concept of "kuchiyose," the art of spirit summoning. Practitioners of kuchiyose call upon the spirits of the departed, seeking their guidance and wisdom. The whispers of these spirits are believed to hold the key to understanding the mysteries of life and death, offering solace and closure to those who seek their counsel. These whispers echo through the stories of Japan, where the boundary between the living and the dead is often fluid and permeable.

In African cultures, whispers are frequently associated with the voices of ancestral spirits, who are believed to guide and protect their descendants. The whispers of these spirits are seen as a source of strength and wisdom, offering insights into the challenges and opportunities that lie ahead. Folklore from various African tribes often features tales of individuals who receive guidance from these whispers, embarking on journeys of self-discovery and transformation. These stories reflect a deep respect for the wisdom of the ancestors and the belief in the continuity of life beyond the physical realm.

The whispers of the Arabian desert tell tales of djinn, supernatural beings who inhabit the unseen corners of the world. These whispers are said to carry the voices of the djinn, who can be both benevolent and malevolent. The tales of the djinn often serve as cautionary tales, warning of the dangers of meddling with forces beyond human understanding. In this cultural context, whispers are a reminder of the vast and mysterious universe that lies beyond human perception, urging humility and respect for the unknown.

In European folklore, whispers are frequently linked to the world of spirits and ghosts. The haunted castles and mist-shrouded moors of Europe are replete with tales of whispers that echo through the corridors of time, carrying the voices of those who have passed on. These whispers are often seen as echoes of unfinished business, urging the living to uncover the truths that lie buried in the past. The whispers of European folklore reflect a fascination with the afterlife and the enduring connection between the living and the dead.

In the vibrant tapestry of Indian culture, whispers are often associated with the concept of "aakashvani," or celestial voices. These whispers are believed to be messages from the gods, offering divine guidance and insight. The stories of aakashvani are woven into the epics and scriptures of India, where whispers play a pivotal role in shaping the destinies of heroes and kings. These tales highlight the belief in a higher cosmic order, where whispers serve as a conduit between the mortal and divine realms.

Amidst these diverse interpretations, one common thread emerges: whispers serve as a bridge between the known and the unknown, the tangible and the intangible. They invite individuals to explore the depths of their own consciousness, to listen to the subtle voices that resonate within the soul. In the realm of folklore, whispers hold the power to transform, to reveal hidden truths, and to illuminate the path of the seeker.

The enduring allure of whispers in cultural folklore lies in their ability to evoke a sense of wonder and mystery. They remind us of the vastness of the universe and the myriad forces that shape our lives, both seen and unseen. In a world where the boundaries between reality and imagination often blur, whispers serve as a reminder of the infinite possibilities that exist beyond the grasp of human understanding.

The Psychological Impact of Whispers

The phenomenon of whispers, especially those that seem to emerge from unknown or invisible sources, has long intrigued psychologists and researchers alike. While whispers can be enchanting and mysterious, they often carry a psychological weight that deeply affects individuals who encounter them. The psychological impact of these whispers can manifest in various ways, from subtle influences on mood and thought to profound effects on mental well-being.

At the core of the psychological impact of phantom whispers is the human tendency to attribute meaning to sounds. The brain is wired to seek patterns and explanations, and when confronted with unexplained whispers, it often strives to make sense of them. This drive to interpret can lead to a range of emotional responses, depending on the context in which the whispers are heard and the individual's personal beliefs and experiences.

For some, whispers evoke a sense of unease or foreboding. The disembodied nature of the sound can trigger feelings of vulnerability or fear, especially if the whispers occur in environments that are already perceived as unsettling. This reaction is rooted in the primal instinct to protect oneself from potential threats, an evolutionary trait that has ensured the survival of the human species. When whispers are perceived as a sign of danger or malevolence, the resulting fear can heighten anxiety levels and contribute to a sense of paranoia.

Conversely, whispers can also elicit feelings of wonder and curiosity. For those who are open to the possibility of the supernatural or the existence of alternate realities, whispers may be seen as a form of communication from these realms. In such cases, the impact of whispers can be positive, sparking a sense of connection to something greater than oneself. This can lead to a heightened sense of spirituality or a deeper appreciation for the mysteries of the universe.

The psychological impact of whispers is also influenced by cultural and personal beliefs. In cultures where whispers are associated with spirits or divine messages, individuals may interpret them as signs of guidance or protection. This cultural framework can provide a sense of comfort and reassurance, mitigating any potential fear or anxiety. Conversely, in cultures where whispers are seen as ominous or malevolent, the psychological impact may be more negative, amplifying feelings of dread or apprehension.

Personal experiences and mental health also play a significant role in shaping an individual's response to whispers. For those with a history of trauma or mental health challenges, whispers may trigger distressing memories or exacerbate symptoms of anxiety or depression. The ambiguity and unpredictability of whispers can be particularly unsettling for individuals who thrive on structure and certainty, leading to increased stress and emotional turmoil.

In some cases, whispers may be perceived as auditory hallucinations, a symptom associated with various mental health disorders. Auditory hallucinations can occur in conditions such as schizophrenia, bipolar disorder, and severe depression, and they often carry significant psychological implications. For individuals experiencing such hallucinations, the whispers can be distressing and disorienting, impacting their ability to function and engage with the world around them.

Despite the potential challenges, whispers can also serve as a catalyst for personal growth and self-discovery. By prompting individuals to confront their fears or explore their beliefs, whispers can encourage introspection and reflection. This process can lead to a deeper understanding of oneself and one's place in the world, fostering resilience and adaptability in the face of life's uncertainties.

For those seeking to navigate the psychological impact of whispers, several strategies may prove beneficial. Cultivating mindfulness and self-awareness can help individuals better understand their emotional responses and manage any distressing feelings that arise. Engaging in practices such as meditation or journaling can provide a safe space for processing thoughts and emotions, allowing individuals to explore the significance of the whispers without becoming overwhelmed.

Building a supportive network of friends, family, or mental health professionals can also be invaluable. Sharing experiences and discussing feelings with others can provide validation and reassurance, helping to alleviate any sense of isolation or confusion. For individuals experiencing distressing auditory hallucinations, seeking professional help is crucial to addressing the underlying mental health concerns and developing effective coping strategies.

Whispers in Literature and Art

Whispers have long captivated the creative imagination, serving as a potent symbol and narrative device in literature and art. Across various mediums, these elusive murmurs embody the intangible, the unseen, and the mysterious, offering endless possibilities for interpretation and exploration. Whispers in literature and art often represent the boundary between the known and unknown, challenging audiences to confront the limits of perception and understanding.

In literature, whispers frequently serve as a metaphor for the subconscious, the hidden desires and fears that reside beneath the surface of consciousness. Authors use whispers to convey the inner voice of their characters, revealing internal conflicts and motivations that drive the narrative forward. This literary device allows readers to delve into the psychological depths of characters, offering insights into their complexities and contradictions.

One of the most iconic examples of whispers in literature can be found in the works of Gothic fiction, where they often signify the presence of supernatural forces or the echoes of past transgressions. In novels like "Jane Eyre" by Charlotte Brontë, whispers add an element of suspense and intrigue, heightening the sense of mystery and foreboding that permeates the narrative. These whispers serve as a reminder of the thin veil between reality and the supernatural, inviting readers to question the nature of truth and perception.

Whispers also play a significant role in the works of modernist writers, who often use them to explore the fragmentation of identity and the complexities of human consciousness. In Virginia Woolf's "Mrs. Dalloway," for example, whispers are used to convey the fleeting thoughts and emotions of characters, capturing the fluid and ephemeral nature of human experience. This narrative technique allows readers to engage with the inner worlds of characters, offering a glimpse into the rich tapestry of thoughts and sensations that shape their reality.

In the realm of poetry, whispers are often employed to evoke a sense of intimacy and introspection. Poets like T.S. Eliot and Sylvia Plath have used whispers to convey the quiet, often unspoken, aspects of human experience, capturing the delicate nuances of emotion and memory. Through the use of whispers, poets can create a sense of immediacy and presence, drawing readers into the intimate world of the speaker.

In visual art, whispers have been depicted through various techniques and styles, often serving as a symbol of mystery and ambiguity. Artists like Edvard Munch and René Magritte have explored the concept of whispers through their surreal and evocative imagery, challenging viewers to engage with the hidden layers of meaning within their work. In Munch's "The Scream," for instance, the swirling lines and distorted forms convey a sense of unease and disquiet, suggesting the whispers of anxiety and existential dread that echo through the human psyche.

Similarly, Magritte's surrealist paintings often feature enigmatic elements that suggest the presence of whispers, inviting viewers to question the nature of reality and perception. In works like "The Lovers," the obscured faces of the figures evoke a sense of mystery and longing, hinting at the unspoken desires and secrets that lie beneath the surface. Through the use of whispers, Magritte's art challenges viewers to confront the complexities of identity and the limitations of perception.

Whispers have also found expression in the world of music, where they are used to convey a sense of intimacy and vulnerability. Composers and musicians often incorporate whispers into their work to create an atmosphere of tension or introspection, drawing listeners into the emotional landscape of the piece. In compositions like Claude Debussy's "Prélude à l'après-midi d'un faune," the use of soft, whispering tones evokes a sense of dreamlike reverie, capturing the ethereal beauty of the natural world.

In contemporary art, whispers continue to inspire and provoke, serving as a catalyst for exploration and experimentation. Artists and writers alike use whispers to challenge conventions and push the boundaries of their medium, inviting audiences to engage with the unknown and embrace the mysteries of existence. Through the use of whispers, contemporary creators can explore themes of identity, memory, and perception, offering new insights into the complexities of the human experience.

The enduring appeal of whispers in literature and art lies in their ability to evoke a sense of wonder and curiosity, drawing audiences into the enigmatic world of the unseen and unheard. By engaging with whispers, creators can explore the depths of the human psyche, revealing the hidden truths and desires that shape our reality. Whether through the written word, visual imagery, or musical composition, whispers continue to captivate and inspire, inviting us to question the nature of existence and the limits of perception.

Real-Life Accounts and Experiences

Whispers are not merely confined to the realms of literature and folklore; they also inhabit the everyday lives of people across the globe. Real-life accounts of whispers often blur the boundaries between reality and imagination, leaving those who experience them both mystified and haunted. These personal narratives offer a unique glimpse into the human encounter with the inexplicable, where whispers serve as a testament to the profound and often unsettling connection between individuals and the unseen world.

One such account comes from a rural village nestled in the heart of Ireland. A woman named Maureen, now in her seventies, recounts a chilling experience from her youth. Late one evening, as she walked home through the dense fog that blanketed the countryside, she heard her name called in a hushed, urgent whisper. The voice was familiar yet unplaceable, echoing in the stillness of the night. Despite her efforts to locate the source, she found herself enveloped in silence. The incident left an indelible mark on Maureen, who interpreted the whisper as a message from her late grandmother, guiding her safely home. This experience became a cherished memory, reinforcing her belief in the enduring presence of loved ones beyond the veil of death.

Similarly, in the bustling city of Tokyo, whispers have become an integral part of the urban landscape. Yuki, a young office worker, describes a recurring phenomenon during her daily commute on the subway. Amidst the clatter of trains and the murmur of passengers, she occasionally hears a soft whisper in her ear, uttering phrases in a language she does not understand. The whispers evoke a sense of familiarity and comfort, as if an unseen companion accompanies her through the crowded city. Despite initial apprehension, Yuki has come to embrace the whispers as a source of solace, a reminder of the unseen connections that bind all people together.

In the American Midwest, whispers have taken on a more ominous tone. A man named Tom recounts an unsettling experience while hiking in the dense forests of his childhood home. As he paused to catch his breath, he heard his own voice whispering from somewhere deep within the woods, urging him to turn back. The eerie familiarity of the voice sent shivers down his spine, compelling him to retreat to the safety of the trailhead. Though he has never been able to explain the incident, Tom remains convinced that the whispers saved him from an unforeseen danger lurking in the forest. This experience has instilled in him a deep respect for the mysteries of the natural world, where whispers serve as a reminder of humanity's vulnerability in the face of the unknown.

In the bustling markets of Marrakech, whispers are woven into the fabric of daily life. A spice vendor named Fatima recounts a series of encounters with whispers that have guided her business decisions for decades. On several occasions, as she stood amidst the vibrant colors and aromas of her market stall, she heard a gentle voice offering advice on which spices to stock and which to avoid. These whispers, which she attributes to the spirits of her ancestors, have consistently proven accurate, bolstering her reputation as a shrewd and successful businesswoman. For Fatima, whispers are a testament to the enduring connection between the past and the present, a reminder that the wisdom of those who came before continues to shape the course of her life.

In the shadowed halls of a centuries-old manor in England, whispers have become an inseparable part of the family legacy. The current owner, Edward, recounts tales passed down through generations of whispered conversations between the house's original inhabitants and their descendants. These whispers, which echo through the corridors during the darkest hours of the night, are said to reveal hidden family secrets and offer guidance during times of turmoil. Edward himself has experienced these whispers, often in moments of solitude when the weight of history feels most palpable. For him, the whispers are a reminder of the enduring presence of the past, a testament to the unbroken chain of family that stretches back through the ages.

These real-life accounts of whispers illustrate the myriad ways in which they manifest in the lives of individuals, transcending cultural and geographical boundaries. Each story offers a unique perspective on the nature of whispers, revealing their capacity to comfort, guide, and challenge those who encounter them. The whispers, whether benevolent or unsettling, serve as a reminder of the vast and mysterious universe that lies beyond the limits of human understanding.

While skeptics may dismiss these accounts as mere auditory hallucinations or the result of overactive imaginations, those who have experienced whispers firsthand often find their lives profoundly altered. For many, whispers spark a sense of wonder and curiosity, prompting them to explore the deeper mysteries of existence and their place within it. These experiences encourage a greater awareness of the interconnectedness of all things, inviting individuals to listen more closely to the subtle voices that resonate within and around them.

Chapter 2: The Unseen World of Spirits

Spirits A Historical Overview

Throughout human history, the concept of spirits has been intricately woven into the fabric of cultures worldwide. These ethereal entities, often seen as intermediaries between the physical and spiritual realms, have captivated the human imagination, serving as both comforters and harbingers of the unknown. A historical overview of spirits reveals a rich tapestry of beliefs and practices, each reflecting the unique worldview and cultural context from which they arise.

In ancient civilizations, spirits were often regarded as divine or semi-divine beings, whose presence was an integral part of the natural world. The Egyptians, for instance, believed in a multitude of spirits that inhabited the earth, sky, and underworld. These spirits were revered as guardians and protectors, maintaining the delicate balance of the cosmos. The "ka" and "ba" were two such spiritual components that defined an individual's essence, believed to persist beyond death. Rituals and offerings ensured the favor of these spirits, securing harmony and prosperity for the living.

The Greeks and Romans also held a profound belief in spirits, often associating them with nature and the elements. Nymphs, dryads, and satyrs were considered spirits of the natural world, inhabiting forests, rivers, and mountains. These spirits were both revered and feared, as their favor could bring bounty and their wrath could invoke disaster. In Roman tradition, the "lares" and "penates" were household spirits, guardians of the home and family, receiving daily offerings as a mark of respect and gratitude.

In the East, the concept of spirits has been central to spiritual and religious practices for millennia. In ancient Chinese culture, spirits were understood as forces that could influence both personal fortunes and the natural world. Ancestor worship played a crucial role, as the spirits of deceased family members were believed to have the ability to guide and protect their descendants. This reverence for ancestral spirits continues to be a fundamental aspect of Chinese spirituality, manifesting in practices such as the Qingming Festival, where families honor their ancestors through rituals and offerings.

In Japan, the Shinto tradition is deeply rooted in the belief in "kami," spirits that inhabit all things, both animate and inanimate. These spirits are considered manifestations of the divine, embodying the essence of nature and humanity. Shrines dedicated to specific kami dot the Japanese landscape, serving as sacred spaces where the living can communicate with the spiritual realm. The reverence for kami underscores a profound respect for the interconnectedness of all life, emphasizing harmony and balance.

The indigenous cultures of Africa have also long held intricate beliefs in spirits, often viewing them as integral to the community and natural world. Spirits are seen as both ancestral and elemental, with rituals and ceremonies designed to honor and appease them.

In many African societies, shamans or spiritual leaders act as intermediaries between the living and the spirit world, facilitating communication and ensuring the well-being of the community. These practices highlight the belief in a dynamic, interconnected universe where spirits play an active role in shaping human destiny.

In the Americas, indigenous peoples have revered spirits as guardians of the land and keepers of wisdom. The Native American cultures, for instance, recognize the presence of spirits in all aspects of the natural world, from animals and plants to rivers and mountains. These spirits are integral to the spiritual and cultural identity of the community, guiding rituals and ceremonies that celebrate the cycles of life and nature. The vision quest, a rite of passage in many Native American traditions, involves seeking the guidance of spirits through solitude and meditation, emphasizing the importance of spiritual connection and self-discovery.

The Middle Ages in Europe ushered in a period of heightened interest in spirits, often intertwined with religious beliefs and practices. The Christian Church acknowledged the existence of spirits, categorizing them as benevolent angels or malevolent demons. The doctrine of purgatory introduced the concept of souls in transition, spirits of the departed seeking redemption before entering heaven. This belief gave rise to various rituals and prayers aimed at aiding these spirits on their journey, a practice that continues in certain Christian traditions.

The Renaissance and Enlightenment periods marked a shift in the perception of spirits, as intellectual curiosity and scientific inquiry began to challenge traditional beliefs. Yet, even as rationalism gained prominence, the fascination with spirits persisted, taking new forms in literature, art, and philosophy. The Romantic era, in particular, saw a resurgence of interest in the supernatural, with spirits becoming central figures in poetry and prose, embodying the mysterious and sublime aspects of nature and the human experience.

In the modern era, the belief in spirits continues to evolve, influenced by cultural exchange and technological advancements. Spiritualism, which emerged in the 19th century, sought to bridge the gap between the living and the spirit world through mediums and séances. This movement gained significant traction, reflecting a growing desire to explore the mysteries of existence and the afterlife. Today, the belief in spirits manifests in various forms, from organized religious practices to personal spiritual beliefs, each reflecting the enduring human quest for understanding and connection.

Types of Spirits Across Cultures

Throughout the world, countless cultures have developed rich tapestries of beliefs concerning spirits, each with its unique classifications and characteristics. The diversity of spirit types across cultures reflects the myriad ways in which humans have sought to understand the unseen forces that influence their lives. These spirits, whether benevolent, malevolent, or neutral, serve as integral components of cultural identity and spiritual practice.

In Africa, spirits are often categorized into ancestral spirits and nature spirits. Ancestral spirits are revered in many African traditions, believed to possess the power to influence the lives of their descendants. They are often honored through rituals and offerings, ensuring the continued favor and protection of the family. Nature spirits, on the other hand, are seen as guardians of the natural world, inhabiting rivers, forests, and mountains. These spirits are often approached with reverence and caution, as their favor can bring prosperity while their wrath may result in calamity.

In Native American cultures, spirits are deeply intertwined with the natural environment. Animal spirits, for example, play a crucial role in many tribal narratives, embodying the qualities and wisdom of the creatures they represent. These spirits act as guides and protectors, offering insight and strength to those who seek their counsel. Additionally, elemental spirits associated with earth, air, fire, and water are often invoked in rituals to maintain harmony and balance within the natural world.

The spirits of East Asia are diverse and multifaceted, reflecting the region's rich spiritual heritage. In Chinese culture, spirits are often categorized into celestial beings, such as dragons and phoenixes, and earthly spirits, like the "hun" and "po," which represent the dual aspects of the human soul. These spirits are integral to various religious and philosophical traditions, influencing concepts of life, death, and rebirth. In Japan, Shinto belief centers around "kami," spirits that inhabit all things. Kami can be ancestors, deities, or natural forces, each with its unique attributes and significance in the spiritual landscape.

In the Indian subcontinent, spirits play a vital role in the tapestry of Hindu, Buddhist, and indigenous beliefs. Hinduism, for example, recognizes a vast pantheon of spirits and deities, each representing different aspects of existence. The "devas" are divine spirits associated with natural and cosmic forces, while "asuras" represent chaos and conflict. In Buddhism, spirits known as "pretas" or hungry ghosts are believed to roam the earth, driven by insatiable desires. These spirits serve as cautionary tales, illustrating the consequences of attachment and craving.

European folklore is replete with spirits that inhabit the liminal spaces between the human and supernatural realms. In Celtic traditions, the "Sidhe" or fairy folk are seen as powerful beings that dwell in the hidden corners of the natural world. These spirits, often portrayed as mischievous and capricious, are both feared and revered. In Norse mythology, spirits known as "landvættir" protect the land and its people, while "draugr," or restless undead, haunt the living with their malevolent presence.

The Islamic world presents a unique perspective on spirits, particularly through the concept of "djinn." These spirits, created from smokeless fire, possess free will and exist in a parallel world to humans. Djinn can be benevolent, malevolent, or neutral, and their interactions with humans are often the subject of cautionary tales and legends. In addition to djinn, Islamic tradition also recognizes angels and demons, each playing distinct roles in the spiritual and moral dimensions of life.

In the Caribbean and Latin America, the fusion of indigenous, African, and European beliefs has given rise to a rich tapestry of spirit types. In Afro-Caribbean religions like Vodou and Santería, spirits known as "loa" or "orishas" are revered as intermediaries between humans and the divine. These spirits possess distinct personalities and domains of influence, guiding practitioners in their spiritual journeys. In indigenous beliefs, spirits known as "duendes" or "aluxes" are seen as protectors of the land, often requiring offerings to maintain their favor.

The diversity of spirit types across cultures highlights the universal human desire to understand and connect with the unseen forces that shape our existence. While each culture possesses its unique classifications and characteristics, common themes emerge, reflecting shared values and concerns. Spirits often serve as guardians, protectors, and guides, embodying the balance between order and chaos, life and death, and the material and spiritual realms.

The belief in spirits also underscores the interconnectedness of all things, inviting individuals to engage with the mysteries of existence and their place within the cosmos. Through rituals, stories, and traditions, spirits become a means of exploring the depths of human experience, offering insights into the complexities of identity, morality, and the human condition.

Communicating with the Invisible

Communication with the invisible world has been a pursuit of humanity for centuries, bridging the tangible and intangible, the seen and unseen. This practice encompasses a wide range of rituals, tools, and beliefs, each reflecting the cultural, spiritual, and personal contexts in which they arise. By exploring these various methods, individuals seek to connect with spirits, ancestors, and otherworldly entities, often in search of guidance, healing, or understanding.

One of the most profound ways people communicate with the invisible is through ritual. Rituals create a sacred space, a liminal zone where the boundaries between worlds become permeable. In many indigenous cultures, shamans or spiritual leaders facilitate this communication, often entering a trance state to serve as intermediaries between their communities and the spirit world. They employ chanting, drumming, and dance to alter their consciousness, enabling them to journey into realms beyond ordinary perception.

In addition to trance, another common practice involves the use of sacred objects. These objects, imbued with spiritual significance, act as conduits for communication. In some African traditions, divination objects like bones or shells are cast and interpreted to convey messages from the spirits.

Similarly, in the Norse tradition, runes are carved and read to seek guidance and insight from the gods and ancestors. These objects serve as tangible links to the intangible, providing a means of deciphering the messages from the invisible world.

Prayer and meditation also play a crucial role in communicating with the invisible. These practices, found in many religious and spiritual traditions, involve focusing one's thoughts and intentions to connect with higher powers or spiritual entities. Prayer can be an invocation, a request for assistance, or a means of expressing gratitude, while meditation often involves quieting the mind to receive insights or messages. Both practices emphasize the importance of intention and sincerity, fostering a deep sense of connection with the divine.

In certain cultures, dreams are considered a vital channel for communication with the invisible. Dreams are seen as a bridge between worlds, a space where spirits and ancestors can convey messages and guidance. In Native American traditions, dream catchers are used to filter out negative dreams, allowing only positive and meaningful visions to pass through. Similarly, in ancient Greek culture, dream incubation involved sleeping in sacred spaces to receive divine messages through dreams. By paying attention to their dreams, individuals can gain insights into their lives and the world around them, often receiving guidance from unseen forces.

Mediumship is another method through which individuals communicate with the invisible. Mediums, believed to possess the ability to connect with spirits, serve as conduits for messages from the other side. This practice gained prominence during the Spiritualist movement of the 19th century, with séances becoming a popular means of contacting the deceased. Mediums often enter a trance state, allowing spirits to communicate through them, offering comfort, closure, and guidance to the living. This form of communication emphasizes the enduring connection between the physical and spiritual realms, offering reassurance that loved ones are never truly gone.

In the realm of technology, modern tools have emerged to facilitate communication with the invisible. Electronic voice phenomena (EVP) and spirit boxes are used by some to capture the voices of spirits, translating their whispers into audible sounds. While skeptics question the validity of these methods, practitioners believe they offer a means of bridging the gap between worlds, providing tangible evidence of the invisible.

Creating an environment conducive to communication with the invisible often involves setting intentions and preparing both the physical and mental space. Cleansing rituals, such as smudging with sage or using protective symbols, are commonly employed to purify the space and invite positive energies. Grounding practices, such as visualization or breathing exercises, help individuals center themselves, fostering a deeper connection with the spiritual realm.

Despite the diversity of methods, communication with the invisible shares common threads: intention, openness, and respect. It requires a willingness to listen and a readiness to embrace the mysteries that lie beyond the visible world. While not every attempt yields clear messages or insights, the process itself can be transformative, fostering a deeper understanding of oneself and the interconnectedness of all things.

However, it is essential to approach communication with the invisible with caution and discernment. Not all entities encountered are benevolent, and it is important to set boundaries and protect oneself from potentially negative influences. Establishing clear intentions and invoking protection through prayers, affirmations, or symbols can help safeguard the practitioner from harm.

For beginners wishing to embark on this journey, starting with simple practices such as meditation or journaling can be an effective way to cultivate a connection with the invisible. Keeping a record of dreams, thoughts, and any messages received can provide valuable insights over time, revealing patterns and themes that may emerge. Additionally, seeking guidance from experienced practitioners or joining a community of like-minded individuals can offer support and encouragement along the path.

The Role of Spirits in Daily Life

The presence of spirits in daily life has been a cornerstone of belief systems around the globe, weaving a rich tapestry of interactions between the tangible and intangible. These interactions manifest in various forms, influencing personal decisions, cultural practices, and communal activities. By examining the role of spirits in everyday existence, one gains insight into how these ethereal entities shape the human experience and foster a deeper connection to the world.

Across diverse cultures, spirits are seen as guardians and protectors, overseeing the well-being of individuals and communities. In many African societies, for instance, ancestral spirits play an integral role in daily life, guiding family members and ensuring harmony within the household. These spirits are believed to watch over their descendants, offering protection and wisdom. Rituals, offerings, and ceremonies are performed regularly to honor these ancestral spirits, fostering a sense of continuity and connection between generations.

In Japan, the presence of spirits, or "kami," permeates daily life, influencing everything from personal decisions to public events. Shinto, the indigenous spirituality of Japan, emphasizes the reverence of kami, which are believed to inhabit all aspects of the natural and human world. Shrines dedicated to specific kami are visited frequently, where individuals offer prayers and seek guidance. This practice underscores the belief in the interconnectedness of all things, with spirits playing an essential role in maintaining balance and harmony.

In the Caribbean, spiritual practices such as Vodou and Santería reflect the daily involvement of spirits in the lives of practitioners. Spirits known as "loa" or "orishas" are considered integral to personal and communal well-being. Practitioners engage with these spirits through rituals, music, and dance, seeking their assistance in matters ranging from health and prosperity to love and conflict resolution. This interaction with spirits is not limited to special occasions but is woven into the fabric of daily life, offering a source of strength and guidance.

In Native American cultures, spirits are deeply embedded in daily life, influencing personal and communal activities. The belief in animal spirits, for example, shapes hunting practices, agricultural cycles, and social rituals. These spirits are seen as teachers and guides, offering wisdom and insight to those who seek their counsel. The presence of spirits in daily life fosters a profound respect for nature and emphasizes the importance of living in harmony with the environment.

In Western cultures, the role of spirits in daily life is often expressed through religious and spiritual practices. Christianity, for instance, acknowledges the presence of angels and saints as intermediaries between God and humanity. These spiritual beings are invoked in prayer and worship, offering protection, guidance, and support. The belief in guardian angels, in particular, underscores the idea that spirits watch over individuals, providing comfort and reassurance in times of need.

Beyond organized religion, many individuals incorporate spiritual practices into their daily routines, seeking connection with spirits through meditation, prayer, or personal rituals. These practices may involve setting intentions, expressing gratitude, or seeking guidance from the spiritual realm. By doing so, individuals cultivate a sense of presence and mindfulness, inviting the influence of spirits into their daily lives.

The role of spirits in daily life extends beyond personal practices, influencing cultural norms and societal values. Festivals, celebrations, and communal rituals often revolve around honoring spirits, reflecting the deep-seated belief in their presence and power. In Mexico, for example, Día de los Muertos, or Day of the Dead, is a vibrant celebration that honors deceased ancestors. Families gather to remember and celebrate the lives of their loved ones, believing that the spirits of the departed return to join in the festivities. This cultural practice highlights the enduring connection between the living and the dead, illustrating how spirits continue to shape the collective identity.

In addition to guiding and protecting, spirits often serve as moral and ethical compasses, influencing behavior and decision-making. In many cultures, spirits are believed to observe and influence human actions, holding individuals accountable for their choices. This belief encourages adherence to cultural norms and values, fostering a sense of responsibility and integrity. The presence of spirits as moral guides underscores the interconnectedness of actions and consequences, emphasizing the importance of living in accordance with spiritual principles.

For many, the role of spirits in daily life offers a source of comfort and reassurance, providing a sense of continuity and connection to something greater than oneself. Whether through personal rituals, communal celebrations, or cultural beliefs, the presence of spirits enriches the human experience, offering guidance, support, and inspiration. By embracing the role of spirits in daily life, individuals and communities cultivate a deeper understanding of their place within the world, fostering harmony and balance in both personal and collective realms.

In modern society, where the pace of life often leads to disconnection from tradition and spirituality, the role of spirits in daily life serves as a reminder of the enduring power of belief and imagination. By acknowledging and honoring the presence of spirits, individuals can reconnect with the intangible aspects of existence, finding meaning and purpose in their daily interactions. This connection to the spiritual realm invites individuals to explore the mysteries of life, to listen to the whispers of the invisible, and to embrace the transformative power of the unseen.

Modern-Day Relevance and Beliefs

In today's fast-paced and technologically driven society, the relevance of spiritual beliefs and practices might initially seem diminished. However, modern-day relevance and beliefs surrounding spirits continue to thrive, adapting to contemporary contexts and fulfilling timeless human needs. As individuals seek meaning, connection, and guidance, the spiritual realm offers a sanctuary of solace and understanding, bridging the gap between the material and the transcendent.

Despite the advances in science and technology, many people still turn to spiritual beliefs as a source of comfort and inspiration. The enduring allure of spiritual practices lies in their ability to address existential questions, offering insights into the nature of life, death, and the universe. For those who find themselves grappling with uncertainty and change, spiritual beliefs provide a framework for understanding the complexities of human existence, fostering a sense of purpose and direction.

The resurgence of interest in spirituality can be seen in the growing popularity of alternative and holistic practices that incorporate spiritual elements. Yoga, meditation, and mindfulness, for example, have become integral parts of many people's lives, blending physical and spiritual well-being. These practices encourage individuals to cultivate awareness and presence, enabling them to connect with their inner selves and the world around them. By embracing the spiritual aspects of these practices, individuals discover a renewed sense of balance and harmony, finding refuge in the sacred amidst the chaos of daily life.

Modern spiritual beliefs often emphasize the importance of personal exploration and individual experience, allowing for a more personalized connection with the spiritual realm. Rather than adhering strictly to dogma or tradition, many people are drawn to eclectic spiritual paths that incorporate diverse influences and practices. This flexibility enables individuals to craft a spiritual journey that resonates with their unique values and beliefs, fostering a deeper sense of authenticity and connection.

The relevance of spiritual beliefs is also evident in the rise of contemporary movements that seek to address the challenges of modern life through spiritual and ethical frameworks. Environmental movements, such as eco-spirituality, emphasize the interconnectedness of all life and the importance of caring for the planet. By integrating spiritual beliefs with environmental activism, these movements inspire individuals to engage in sustainable practices and advocate for the well-being of the earth and its inhabitants.

In addition to personal and environmental contexts, spiritual beliefs continue to play a significant role in social and cultural life. Communities around the world celebrate traditional festivals, rituals, and ceremonies that honor spiritual beliefs and foster a sense of belonging and identity. These events provide opportunities for individuals to connect with their cultural heritage, reinforcing the values and traditions that shape their lives. By participating in these communal expressions of spirituality, individuals experience a sense of unity and continuity, drawing strength from their shared beliefs and experiences.

The digital age has also transformed the ways in which spiritual beliefs are expressed and shared. Online platforms and social media have become vibrant spaces for spiritual exploration and connection, enabling individuals to access a wealth of information and resources. Virtual communities and forums offer support and guidance, fostering a sense of community among those seeking spiritual growth.

This digital landscape allows for the exchange of ideas and practices, bridging geographical and cultural divides and enriching the global tapestry of spiritual beliefs.

As people continue to navigate the complexities of the modern world, spiritual beliefs provide a source of resilience and strength. In times of crisis and uncertainty, individuals often turn to their spiritual beliefs for comfort and guidance, drawing on the wisdom and support of the spiritual realm. Whether through prayer, meditation, or ritual, these practices offer a sense of stability and hope, reminding individuals of their connection to something greater than themselves.

The modern-day relevance of spiritual beliefs is further reflected in the increasing interest in practices such as mediumship and channeling, which seek to connect with the spiritual realm. These practices, once considered fringe or unconventional, have gained a wider audience as individuals seek to explore the mysteries of existence and the afterlife. By engaging with the spiritual realm, individuals hope to gain insights into their lives, heal from past traumas, and find closure and peace.

Incorporating spiritual beliefs into daily life also fosters a sense of mindfulness and intentionality, encouraging individuals to live with greater awareness and compassion. By cultivating a spiritual practice, individuals can develop a deeper understanding of themselves and their relationships, enhancing their ability to navigate the challenges of modern life with grace and resilience.

The continued relevance of spiritual beliefs in contemporary society underscores the enduring power of the human spirit. As individuals seek to understand their place in the world, spiritual beliefs offer a guiding light, illuminating the path to self-discovery and transformation. By embracing the spiritual dimensions of existence, individuals can cultivate a rich and meaningful life, grounded in connection, purpose, and love.

Scientific Perspectives on Spirits

The intersection between science and spirituality often raises intriguing questions about the nature of existence and the unseen forces that many believe shape our lives. Scientific perspectives on spirits can appear to be at odds with traditional spiritual beliefs, yet they offer a fascinating lens through which to explore the mysteries of the unseen. By examining the scientific approach, one gains insight into how modern understanding attempts to unravel the complexities of phenomena often associated with spirits.

Science, rooted in empirical evidence and rigorous methodology, seeks to explain the world through observation and experimentation. When faced with claims of spirits or spiritual phenomena, scientists typically approach the subject with skepticism, demanding evidence that can be tested and replicated. This skepticism stems not from a dismissal of spirituality, but rather from a commitment to understanding the natural world through observable data.

One area where science has intersected with spiritual beliefs is in the study of near-death experiences (NDEs). These experiences, reported by individuals who have come close to death, often include visions of bright lights, tunnels, or encounters with deceased loved ones. While some interpret these experiences as evidence of an afterlife, scientists have sought to understand them through the lens of neurology and psychology. Research suggests that NDEs may be linked to changes in brain activity, neurotransmitter release, or oxygen deprivation, offering a physiological explanation for these profound experiences.

Similarly, the phenomenon of sleep paralysis has been examined by scientists seeking to understand its connection to reports of spiritual encounters. During sleep paralysis, individuals may experience vivid hallucinations, often involving a sense of presence or malevolent entities. While some cultures interpret these experiences as interactions with spirits or demons, scientific research attributes them to a disruption in the sleep cycle, where the mind remains partially awake while the body is immobile. This research highlights the complex interplay between the brain and perception, offering insights into experiences often attributed to spiritual encounters.

The scientific exploration of consciousness also intersects with spiritual beliefs, particularly in the study of altered states of consciousness. Practices such as meditation, trance, or the use of psychoactive substances have been shown to induce altered states that many interpret as spiritual or mystical experiences. Neuroscientists have studied these states to understand their impact on brain function, revealing changes in neural connectivity and brain wave patterns. This research suggests that spiritual experiences may arise from specific neurological processes, offering a potential bridge between the material and the spiritual.

Quantum physics, with its exploration of the fundamental nature of reality, has also sparked interest in the scientific community regarding the existence of spirits or other dimensions. Concepts such as quantum entanglement and the multiverse theory challenge traditional notions of space and time, suggesting that reality may be far more complex than previously understood. While these theories do not provide direct evidence of spirits, they open the door to possibilities beyond the observable universe, inviting speculation about the nature of consciousness and existence.

Parapsychology, a field dedicated to studying psychic phenomena, further explores the potential scientific basis for spiritual experiences. Researchers in this field investigate claims of telepathy, precognition, and psychokinesis, often associated with spiritual or supernatural abilities. While mainstream science remains skeptical of these claims, parapsychologists continue to conduct experiments and collect data, seeking to understand the potential mechanisms underlying these phenomena.

In addition to these scientific explorations, the study of cultural anthropology provides valuable insights into the role of spirits and spiritual beliefs across societies. Anthropologists examine how different cultures interpret spiritual phenomena, revealing the diverse ways in which humans have sought to understand the unseen. This cross-cultural perspective highlights the universality of spiritual beliefs, suggesting that the human experience of spirits may be deeply rooted in the shared psyche.

Despite the scientific community's cautious approach to spiritual phenomena, there is an ongoing dialogue between science and spirituality. Some scientists and spiritual practitioners advocate for an integrative approach, seeking to bridge the gap between empirical evidence and spiritual experience. This dialogue encourages a broader understanding of the human experience, acknowledging the limitations of both scientific and spiritual perspectives.

For beginners interested in exploring the scientific perspectives on spirits, it is important to approach the subject with an open mind and a critical eye. Engaging with scientific literature, attending lectures, or participating in discussions can provide a deeper understanding of the empirical approach to spiritual phenomena. By examining the evidence and considering multiple viewpoints, individuals can develop a nuanced perspective that respects both scientific inquiry and spiritual belief.

Chapter 3: The Veil Between Worlds

Understanding the Concept of the Veil

The concept of the veil has captivated the human imagination for centuries, serving as a metaphorical boundary that separates the physical world from the spiritual. This enigmatic barrier, often depicted as a thin, translucent curtain, symbolizes the division between the known and the unknown, the seen and the unseen. By examining the notion of the veil, individuals can gain insight into the ways in which different cultures and belief systems interpret the mysteries of existence.

In many spiritual traditions, the veil is believed to be a mutable boundary, one that can be traversed or lifted under certain circumstances. This permeability allows for communication and interaction between realms, enabling individuals to access spiritual insights, guidance, and healing. The idea that the veil can be thinned or parted is central to rituals and practices designed to connect with the spiritual realm, such as meditation, prayer, or trance work.

One of the most profound interpretations of the veil comes from the ancient Celts, who believed that the veil between the worlds was thinnest during Samhain, a festival marking the transition from harvest to winter. During this time, it was thought that the spirits of the dead could more easily cross into the living world. This belief fostered rituals of remembrance and communication with ancestors, emphasizing the cyclical nature of life and death and the enduring connection between generations.

Similarly, in many indigenous cultures, the veil is seen as a dynamic boundary that can be traversed by shamans or spiritual leaders. These individuals, through the use of altered states of consciousness, serve as intermediaries between the physical and spiritual worlds. By journeying beyond the veil, shamans seek to bring back knowledge, healing, and guidance for their communities. This practice underscores the belief in the interconnectedness of all things and the fluid nature of reality.

In Eastern philosophies, the concept of the veil is often associated with the illusion of separation and the pursuit of enlightenment. In Hindu and Buddhist traditions, the veil, or "maya," represents the illusory nature of the material world, obscuring the true essence of reality. Through spiritual practices such as meditation and mindfulness, individuals strive to see beyond the veil of illusion, attaining a state of enlightenment where the unity of all existence is revealed.

The veil is also a prominent theme in Western esoteric traditions, where it is often depicted as a barrier that can be pierced through spiritual awakening and self-discovery. In the Hermetic and mystical traditions, the veil symbolizes the hidden knowledge and truths that lie beyond ordinary perception. Initiates are encouraged to lift the veil through study, contemplation, and inner transformation, revealing the deeper mysteries of the universe.

For those seeking to understand the concept of the veil, it is essential to approach the subject with an open mind and a willingness to explore diverse perspectives. Engaging with the teachings and practices of different spiritual traditions can offer valuable insights into the nature of the veil and the ways in which it influences human experience.

In practical terms, individuals can cultivate a deeper understanding of the veil by incorporating spiritual practices into their daily lives. Meditation, for example, serves as a powerful tool for quieting the mind and expanding awareness, allowing individuals to glimpse beyond the veil and access the wisdom of the spiritual realm. By setting aside time for reflection and introspection, individuals can cultivate a sense of presence and connection, inviting the influence of the unseen into their lives.

Dreamwork is another effective means of exploring the concept of the veil, as dreams are often considered a bridge between worlds. By keeping a dream journal and paying attention to the symbols and messages that arise during sleep, individuals can gain insights into their subconscious minds and the spiritual forces that may be at play. This practice encourages a deeper understanding of the self and the interconnectedness of all things.

Rituals and ceremonies also provide opportunities to engage with the concept of the veil. Whether through solitary or communal practices, rituals create a sacred space where the boundaries between worlds can be more easily navigated. By setting intentions and invoking spiritual energies, individuals can foster a sense of connection and communion with the unseen, drawing strength and guidance from the spiritual realm.

The concept of the veil invites individuals to embrace the mysteries of existence and to explore the depths of their own spirituality. By acknowledging the presence of the veil and its influence on human experience, individuals can cultivate a greater sense of wonder and curiosity, questioning the nature of reality and their place within it. This exploration encourages a deeper understanding of the self and the universe, fostering a sense of unity and interconnectedness with all that is.

In a world often driven by material concerns and external validation, the concept of the veil serves as a reminder of the intangible aspects of existence that lie beyond the surface. By embracing the mysteries of the veil and seeking to understand its significance, individuals can cultivate a richer and more meaningful life, grounded in the exploration of the inner and outer worlds.

Mythological Significance of the Veil

The veil, a symbol shrouded in mystery and enchantment, has captivated human imagination across cultures and epochs. Its mythological significance is profound, representing the boundary between the known and the unknown, the mortal and the divine. This enigmatic barrier appears in countless myths and legends, where it serves as both a protective shield and a gateway to otherworldly realms. By delving into the mythological significance of the veil, we uncover the rich tapestry of stories and beliefs that have shaped human understanding of the cosmos.

In ancient Greek mythology, the veil is often associated with the goddess Hecate, the guardian of thresholds and the crossroads of life and death. Hecate's veil symbolizes her dominion over the boundaries between worlds, granting her the power to guide souls through the underworld. This imagery reflects the belief in the veil as a liminal space, where the ordinary and the extraordinary converge. Hecate's role as a psychopomp underscores the veil's function as a bridge between the living and the dead, a theme that recurs in numerous mythological traditions.

Similarly, the veil features prominently in the mythology of ancient Egypt, where it is linked to the goddess Isis. As the mother of Horus and the wife of Osiris, Isis is often depicted with a veil that conceals her divine mysteries. The lifting of her veil is said to reveal hidden knowledge and the secrets of the universe. This association highlights the veil's role as a symbol of divine wisdom and the transformative power of revelation. The myth of Isis and Osiris, with its themes of death and rebirth, echoes the veil's function as a boundary between life and the afterlife.

In Norse mythology, the veil appears in the form of the Bifröst, the rainbow bridge that connects the realm of the gods, Asgard, with the world of humans, Midgard. The Bifröst is both a pathway and a barrier, safeguarding the divine realm from mortal intrusion while allowing select individuals to traverse its arches. This mythological construct emphasizes the veil's dual nature as both a protective shield and a conduit for spiritual ascent. The Bifröst, shimmering with all the colors of the rainbow, symbolizes the spectrum of possibilities that lie beyond the veil, inviting heroes and seekers to embark on epic quests of discovery.

The veil's mythological significance extends to the Hindu tradition, where it is embodied in the concept of "maya," the cosmic illusion that obscures the true nature of reality. In Hindu cosmology, maya is the veil that separates the finite world of appearances from the infinite realm of the absolute. The lifting of this veil is achieved through spiritual practices that lead to enlightenment and the realization of one's divine essence. This notion of the veil as an illusionary barrier resonates with the idea of spiritual awakening and the quest for ultimate truth.

In Celtic mythology, the veil is intricately woven into the fabric of the Otherworld, a mystical realm inhabited by fairies, spirits, and deities. The Celtic festival of Samhain, marking the end of the harvest season, is believed to be a time when the veil between the worlds is at its thinnest. During Samhain, the spirits of the dead are thought to return to the mortal realm, and humans can more easily access the Otherworld. This concept of a thinning veil underscores the cyclical nature of time and the interconnectedness of all existence. The stories of heroes who journey into the Otherworld to gain wisdom or retrieve lost souls highlight the veil's role as a portal to the unknown.

The veil's mythological significance is further enriched by its presence in Judeo-Christian traditions. In the Bible, the veil of the temple in Jerusalem serves as a barrier separating the Holy of Holies, the innermost sanctum where the divine presence resides, from the rest of the temple. The tearing of this veil at the moment of Christ's death symbolizes the removal of the barrier between humanity and the divine, signifying the possibility of direct communion with God. This powerful image conveys the veil's role as both a separator and a unifier, bridging the gap between the human and the sacred.

Across these diverse mythological landscapes, the veil emerges as a symbol of profound significance, embodying the mysteries and wonders that lie beyond the limits of human perception. Its presence in myth and legend speaks to the universal human desire to transcend the ordinary and explore the extraordinary. By engaging with the mythological significance of the veil, individuals can gain a deeper understanding of the timeless themes that have shaped human consciousness and continue to inspire the quest for knowledge and meaning.

In practical terms, exploring the mythological significance of the veil can enrich one's spiritual practice and personal growth. By reflecting on the stories and symbols associated with the veil, individuals can cultivate a sense of wonder and curiosity, inviting the mysteries of existence into their lives. Engaging with mythological narratives can also offer valuable insights into the archetypal patterns that underlie human experience, fostering a deeper connection to the collective unconscious and the shared heritage of humanity.

Rituals to Pierce the Veil

Throughout history, rituals have served as powerful tools for transcending the ordinary and accessing the spiritual realms that lie beyond the veil. These ceremonies, imbued with symbolism and intention, provide a structured means for individuals to connect with the unseen and invite the influence of the divine into their lives. By understanding and practicing these rituals, individuals can cultivate a deeper sense of connection and insight, piercing the veil that separates the material world from the spiritual.

One of the most enduring rituals designed to pierce the veil is the use of sacred circles, often employed in various spiritual traditions as a means of creating a protected and focused space for spiritual work. The circle symbolizes wholeness and unity, serving as a microcosm of the universe. Within its boundaries, practitioners engage in meditation, prayer, or invocation, seeking to connect with spiritual forces or entities. The circle acts as both a conduit and a shield, allowing energies to flow while safeguarding against unwanted influences.

The preparation and creation of a sacred circle can be a ritual in itself, involving the use of salt, herbs, or other symbolic items to cleanse and sanctify the space. By setting clear intentions and invoking protective energies, individuals can create an environment conducive to spiritual exploration and communion. As the circle is cast, practitioners may call upon guiding spirits, deities, or ancestors, inviting their presence and wisdom to guide the ritual.

Another powerful ritual to pierce the veil involves the use of candles and fire. Light has long been associated with the divine and the illumination of hidden truths. The act of lighting a candle can serve as a symbolic gesture of inviting clarity and insight, dispelling the shadows that obscure understanding. During these rituals, individuals may focus on the flame, using it as a focal point for meditation or visualization. As the candle burns, intentions and prayers are carried upward, transcending the veil and reaching the spiritual realm.

The choice of candle color can also enhance the ritual's purpose, with specific hues corresponding to different energies or intentions. White candles, for example, are often used for purity and protection, while blue candles may be chosen for communication and spiritual insight. By aligning the ritual's elements with the practitioner's goals, the act of candle lighting becomes a powerful tool for transformation and connection.

Herbal and incense rituals offer another means of piercing the veil, harnessing the power of nature's gifts to facilitate spiritual communication. The use of specific herbs and resins, such as sage, frankincense, or myrrh, has been revered for their cleansing and elevating properties. When burned, these substances release aromatic smoke, believed to purify the space and elevate the practitioner's consciousness.

Incorporating herbal elements into rituals can involve creating bundles or smudges, which are lit and used to waft smoke around the body or ritual space. The act of smudging serves not only to cleanse but also to invite protective energies and enhance spiritual awareness. By focusing on the fragrance and observing the movement of the smoke, individuals can enter a meditative state, opening themselves to insights and messages from the spiritual realm.

Chanting and sound rituals utilize the power of vibration and resonance to pierce the veil, aligning the practitioner's energy with higher frequencies. The use of mantras, chants, or singing bowls can create a sonic landscape that facilitates altered states of consciousness, allowing individuals to transcend ordinary perception. Sound has the unique ability to bypass the intellect, reaching deep into the subconscious and connecting with the spiritual essence.

When engaging in sound rituals, practitioners may repeat specific chants or phrases, focusing on their intention and allowing the sound to reverberate within their being. The repetition and rhythm of the chant serve to quiet the mind and elevate the spirit, creating a pathway through the veil. Singing bowls, gongs, or other instruments can be used to enhance the ritual, their tones resonating with the body's energy centers and promoting balance and harmony.

Dreamwork rituals offer another avenue for piercing the veil, exploring the rich symbolism and messages that emerge from the subconscious during sleep. By setting intentions before sleep and keeping a dream journal, individuals can cultivate a greater awareness of their dream states, inviting insights and guidance from the spiritual realm. The act of recording dreams encourages reflection and analysis, allowing patterns and themes to emerge over time.

Incorporating dreamwork into a spiritual practice involves creating a bedtime ritual that includes relaxation techniques, meditation, or the use of herbal teas to promote restful sleep. By focusing on a specific question or intention before sleep, individuals can invite the dream world to offer answers and insights. Upon waking, the immediate recording of dreams helps to capture the fleeting details and emotions, providing a rich tapestry for exploration and understanding.

Each of these rituals offers a unique pathway for engaging with the spiritual realm, inviting individuals to pierce the veil and explore the mysteries that lie beyond. By approaching these practices with intention, respect, and an open heart, individuals can cultivate a deeper connection to the divine, enriching their lives with wisdom and insight.

Stories of Veil Crossings

The allure of crossing the veil has long been a source of fascination, inspiring a wealth of stories that explore the boundary between the physical and the spiritual. These narratives often feature individuals who venture into the unknown, seeking wisdom, adventure, or transformation. Each tale offers a glimpse into the mysteries that lie beyond the veil, illuminating the profound connections between the seen and the unseen.

One of the most enduring stories of veil crossings comes from the Celtic tradition, where the legendary hero Cú Chulainn embarks on a journey into the Otherworld. Guided by a mysterious woman who appears at the edge of a sacred grove, Cú Chulainn is drawn into a realm of enchantment and danger. As he navigates the Otherworld, he encounters legendary creatures and faces trials that test his courage and resolve. These experiences grant him insights and abilities that he carries back to the mortal world, enriching his life and legacy. This tale illustrates the transformative power of crossing the veil, where the journey itself becomes a catalyst for personal growth and understanding.

In Greek mythology, Orpheus stands as a poignant figure whose story of veil crossing resonates with themes of love and loss. When his beloved Eurydice dies, Orpheus ventures into the underworld, determined to bring her back. Armed only with his lyre and his enchanting voice, he charms the gods of the underworld, gaining permission to lead Eurydice back to the world of the living. Yet, the journey is fraught with peril, for Orpheus must not look back until they have both crossed the threshold. Overcome with doubt and longing, he falters just before reaching the surface, and Eurydice is lost to him forever. This tale underscores the bittersweet nature of crossing the veil, where the quest for reunion ultimately results in profound self-discovery and acceptance.

The story of Inanna, the Sumerian goddess of love and war, offers another powerful narrative of veil crossing. Inanna descends into the underworld to visit her sister Ereshkigal, the goddess of death. As she passes through each of the seven gates, she is stripped of her royal garments and symbols of power, arriving naked and vulnerable before her sister. Inanna's journey into the underworld represents a symbolic death and rebirth, where she confronts the shadow aspects of her being. Through her trials, she gains a deeper understanding of herself and the cyclical nature of life and death. Her eventual return to the world of the living signifies a renewal of life and fertility, illustrating the regenerative power of crossing the veil.

In Norse mythology, the tale of Odin's quest for wisdom exemplifies the theme of veil crossing as a pursuit of knowledge. Odin, the Allfather, seeks to gain the wisdom of the runes, mystical symbols that hold the secrets of the universe. To acquire this knowledge, he sacrifices himself by hanging from the World Tree, Yggdrasil, for nine days and nights, wounded and alone. In this liminal state between life and death, Odin gains the insight he seeks, emerging with newfound understanding and power. This story highlights the willingness to endure hardship and sacrifice in the pursuit of enlightenment, where crossing the veil becomes a transformative rite of passage.

The Native American tale of the Dreamtime explores the veil crossing as a means of connecting with the spiritual essence of the land. In this tradition, the Dreamtime represents a primordial era when ancestral spirits shaped the earth and its inhabitants.

By entering a dream state, individuals can commune with these spirits, gaining guidance and wisdom for themselves and their communities. The journey into the Dreamtime is a sacred act of crossing the veil, where the boundaries between past and present, and between the physical and spiritual realms, dissolve. This narrative emphasizes the interconnectedness of all things and the importance of maintaining harmony with the natural world.

In modern times, stories of near-death experiences (NDEs) have captured the imagination of those curious about veil crossings. Individuals who have come close to death often describe vivid encounters with bright lights, tunnels, or deceased loved ones. These experiences, though diverse, share common elements that suggest a journey beyond the veil. Many who have undergone NDEs report a sense of profound peace and interconnectedness, returning to life with altered perspectives and a renewed sense of purpose. These contemporary narratives offer insights into the nature of consciousness and the possibility of existence beyond the physical body.

The tales of veil crossings, whether ancient or modern, share a common thread of transformation and revelation. They invite individuals to embark on journeys of exploration, challenging them to confront their fears and transcend their limitations. By engaging with these stories, one can gain a deeper appreciation for the mysteries of life and the potential for growth and understanding that lies beyond the veil.

For those interested in exploring the concept of veil crossings in their own lives, storytelling can serve as a powerful tool for reflection and insight. By crafting personal narratives that draw on the themes and symbols of veil crossings, individuals can explore their own journeys of self-discovery and transformation. These stories can be shared with others, fostering a sense of connection and community while honoring the timeless tradition of storytelling.

The stories of veil crossings remind us of the infinite possibilities that exist beyond the boundaries of our perception. They encourage us to embrace the unknown, to seek wisdom and truth in the hidden corners of our existence. Through these narratives, we are invited to transcend the limitations of the material world, to journey into the realms of the spirit, and to return enriched and enlightened by the experience.

The Veil in Popular Culture

The veil, as a concept, has permeated popular culture, serving as a compelling symbol in literature, film, music, and visual arts. Its allure lies in its ability to evoke mystery and allure while simultaneously acting as a barrier that conceals deeper truths. Through its various representations, the veil captures the imagination of audiences, inviting them to explore the boundaries between reality and fantasy, perception and illusion.

In literature, the veil often serves as a metaphor for hidden knowledge or forbidden truths. One of the most notable examples is Nathaniel Hawthorne's short story "The Minister's Black Veil," where Reverend Hooper dons a black veil that shrouds his face, unsettling his congregation and sparking contemplation about the nature of sin and guilt. The veil becomes a symbol of the secrets that lie beneath the surface, suggesting that everyone carries hidden burdens. This narrative invites readers to reflect on the complexities of human nature and the facades people maintain.

In the realm of fantasy and science fiction, the veil is frequently depicted as a threshold to alternate dimensions or realities. This theme is explored in Philip Pullman's "His Dark Materials" trilogy, where the character Lyra Belacqua embarks on a journey to explore parallel universes. The "subtle knife" allows characters to cut through the fabric of reality, crossing the veil to discover new worlds. This depiction of the veil as a gateway to the unknown captivates readers, offering a sense of adventure and the possibility of uncovering profound truths.

Film and television have also embraced the veil as a powerful visual and narrative device. In the movie "The Others," the veil takes on a literal form as curtains that block out the light, creating an atmosphere of suspense and uncertainty. The film's protagonist, Grace, gradually uncovers the truth of her existence, as the veil between the living and the dead is lifted. The use of the veil in this context highlights themes of revelation and the blurred boundaries between life and death, challenging viewers to question their perceptions of reality.

The Harry Potter series by J.K. Rowling features the veil in the form of the mysterious archway in the Department of Mysteries. This archway, shrouded in whispers, symbolizes the boundary between life and death. The tragic moment when Sirius Black passes through the veil underscores the finality and mystery of death, leaving both characters and readers to grapple with the emotions and uncertainties that accompany loss. The veil's presence in this series serves as a poignant reminder of the unknown that awaits beyond the mortal realm.

Music, too, has drawn inspiration from the concept of the veil, using it as a metaphor for emotional depth and introspection. The song "Behind the Veil" by Dream Theater explores themes of self-discovery and the search for hidden truths. The lyrics suggest that understanding oneself requires peeling back layers and confronting the shadows that reside within. The veil becomes a symbol of the barriers people erect to protect themselves, yet it also represents the potential for growth and transformation when those barriers are overcome.

Visual arts have captured the enigmatic allure of the veil through painting and photography, using it to evoke a sense of mystery and beauty. The works of artists like René Magritte often feature veiled figures, challenging viewers to question the nature of identity and reality. In Magritte's "The Lovers," a couple kisses while their faces are obscured by cloth, creating a paradox of intimacy and concealment. The veil in this context suggests that true understanding may remain elusive, even in moments of closeness.

In contemporary fashion, the veil has made a resurgence as both a statement piece and a cultural symbol. Designers incorporate veils into their collections, playing with notions of tradition and modernity, visibility and obscurity. The veil's presence on the runway invites audiences to consider its historical and cultural significance, as well as its role in shaping identity and self-expression. This fusion of fashion and symbolism highlights the veil's versatility and its enduring impact on cultural narratives.

The veil's presence in popular culture extends to the realm of digital media and gaming, where it serves as a narrative device and a visual motif. In video games like "The Legend of Zelda: Twilight Princess," the veil is represented as a twilight realm that players must navigate. This journey through the veil involves confronting challenges and uncovering hidden truths, mirroring the hero's quest for understanding and enlightenment. The use of the veil in gaming underscores its capacity to create immersive experiences that invite players to explore new dimensions.

The enduring appeal of the veil in popular culture lies in its ability to evoke emotion, curiosity, and introspection. It serves as a versatile symbol that can be adapted to various contexts, offering rich opportunities for storytelling and artistic expression. By engaging with the veil's representations in literature, film, music, and art, audiences are invited to embark on a journey of exploration and discovery, questioning the boundaries of perception and reality.

Chapter 4: The Language of Whispers

Decoding the Messages

Decoding the messages that traverse the veil requires a keen sense of intuition and a willingness to engage deeply with the symbols and signs present in our lives. These messages, often subtle and elusive, can manifest in dreams, synchronicities, or sudden insights, offering guidance and wisdom from the unseen realms. By developing the skills to interpret these messages, individuals can unlock a profound connection to the spiritual dimensions and navigate their life's journey with greater clarity and purpose.

One of the most accessible ways to begin decoding the messages is by paying attention to dreams. Dreams serve as a rich tapestry of the subconscious, weaving together personal experiences, emotions, and symbols that may convey significant insights. Keeping a dream journal is an invaluable practice for capturing the details of dreams, which can otherwise fade quickly upon waking. By recording dreams immediately, individuals can preserve the vivid imagery and emotions, providing a foundation for reflection and interpretation.

When decoding the messages within dreams, it is essential to recognize that symbols often carry both personal and universal meanings. A recurring image in a dream might have a unique significance to the dreamer, tied to their personal history or experiences. For example, a childhood home appearing in dreams could represent security or unresolved issues from the past. Conversely, certain archetypal symbols, such as water representing emotions or a journey symbolizing life transitions, may hold broader interpretations.

To fully understand the messages in dreams, individuals should consider the context and emotions associated with each dream. Questions such as "How did I feel during the dream?" and "What events in my life might relate to the dream's themes?" can provide valuable insights. By exploring these aspects, dreamers can decode the messages and uncover the guidance or warnings embedded within their subconscious narratives.

Another avenue for decoding messages involves observing synchronicities, those meaningful coincidences that seem to defy logical explanation. These occurrences often serve as signs that individuals are aligned with their spiritual path or need to pay attention to specific aspects of their lives. For example, repeatedly encountering a particular animal or number may indicate a message from the universe, urging reflection on its significance.

To interpret the messages in synchronicities, individuals can start by noticing patterns and recurring themes in their lives. Keeping a journal of these events can help identify connections and meanings that may not be immediately apparent. It is also helpful to research the symbolic meanings associated with certain animals, numbers, or objects, as these can provide additional layers of understanding.

In addition to dreams and synchronicities, messages from the veil can manifest as sudden insights or intuitive feelings. These moments of clarity often arise unexpectedly and can offer profound guidance or solutions to challenges. Cultivating a practice of mindfulness and meditation can enhance one's ability to receive and interpret these messages, allowing for a clearer connection to the intuitive mind.

When faced with an intuitive insight, it is important to trust and honor the message, even if it contradicts rational thought. Intuition operates beyond the confines of logic, drawing from a deeper well of wisdom and understanding. By embracing these insights, individuals can make informed decisions that align with their true selves and life purpose.

Engaging with divination tools, such as tarot cards or runes, can also facilitate the process of decoding messages. These tools serve as mirrors to the subconscious, providing visual and symbolic cues that can illuminate aspects of one's life. When used with intention and respect, divination can offer clarity and perspective, helping individuals gain a deeper understanding of the messages they receive.

In practice, working with divination involves setting a clear intention and approaching the process with an open mind and heart. As individuals draw cards or cast runes, they should reflect on the imagery and symbolism presented, considering how it relates to their current situation or question. The interpretation may not always be straightforward, but by engaging with the process and trusting their intuition, individuals can uncover the messages that are most relevant to their journey.

Connecting with nature provides another powerful means of decoding messages from the veil. Nature is a reflection of the divine, offering countless opportunities to receive guidance through its rhythms and cycles. Observing the behavior of animals, the changing seasons, or the growth of plants can provide insights into one's own life and spiritual path.

By spending time in nature, individuals can attune themselves to the natural world and its messages. Practices such as grounding, where one connects physically and energetically with the earth, can enhance this connection. As individuals immerse themselves in the natural environment, they may find that messages from the veil become more apparent, offering guidance and inspiration.

Symbolism in Whispers

The whispers that drift through the veil often carry with them a rich tapestry of symbolism, weaving together the seen and unseen in a dance of meaning and mystery. These whispers, subtle yet profound, offer insights and guidance, encouraging those who listen to delve deeper into their own consciousness and the world around them. Understanding the symbolism in these whispers can provide a framework for personal growth and spiritual exploration, allowing individuals to navigate their lives with greater awareness and intention.

Symbols have long been used as a means of communication, transcending language and cultural barriers to convey universal truths and archetypal themes. When whispers emerge, they often do so through symbols that resonate on both a personal and collective level. These symbols may appear in dreams, meditation, or moments of stillness, inviting reflection and interpretation.

One of the most potent symbols often found in whispers is the labyrinth. Unlike a maze, which is designed to confuse, a labyrinth offers a single path leading to the center and back out again. It symbolizes a journey inward, where one confronts their own truths and emerges transformed. When whispers speak of a labyrinth, they may be encouraging an exploration of the self, a journey through the layers of one's psyche to uncover hidden insights and wisdom.

The tree, with its roots deep in the earth and branches reaching toward the sky, is another powerful symbol frequently encountered in whispers. It represents growth, stability, and the connection between the physical and spiritual realms. Trees often appear in whispers as reminders to remain grounded while reaching for higher understanding. They encourage individuals to nurture their roots—whether through family, community, or personal values—while aspiring to greater heights of consciousness.

Animals, too, play a significant role in the symbolism of whispers. Each creature carries its own unique qualities and messages, often reflecting aspects of the human experience. The owl, for instance, is a symbol of wisdom and intuition. Its presence in whispers may suggest the need to trust one's inner knowledge and to look beyond the surface for deeper truths. Similarly, the butterfly, with its transformative journey from caterpillar to chrysalis to winged beauty, often symbolizes change and personal evolution. When butterflies appear in whispers, they may be encouraging acceptance and embrace of life's transitions.

Water, in its various forms, is a symbol of emotion, intuition, and the subconscious. Whispers that speak of rivers, oceans, or rain may be calling attention to one's emotional state or urging a deeper exploration of intuitive insights. Water's ability to flow and adapt serves as a reminder of the importance of flexibility and resilience in the face of life's challenges.

Numbers also hold significant symbolic meaning in whispers, often reflecting patterns or cycles. The number three, for instance, is associated with balance and harmony, representing the union of mind, body, and spirit. When this number appears in whispers, it may be signaling the need for alignment and integration of these aspects. The number seven, often seen as mystical or spiritual, is linked to introspection and the quest for truth. Whispers that present the number seven may be guiding individuals to seek deeper understanding and spiritual growth.

Colors, too, carry symbolic weight in whispers, conveying emotions and states of being. The color blue, for instance, is often associated with tranquility and communication. Whispers that bring forth blue may be encouraging calmness and clarity in expression. Red, on the other hand, symbolizes passion and vitality, urging action and energy. When red appears in whispers, it may be calling for courage and assertiveness in pursuing one's goals.

Interpreting the symbolism in whispers requires a willingness to engage with one's own intuition and experiences. It involves an openness to the messages that emerge, as well as a readiness to explore their meanings within the context of one's life. By reflecting on the symbols and their potential interpretations, individuals can gain valuable insights and guidance, empowering them to make informed decisions and embrace their spiritual journey.

To deepen the understanding of symbolism in whispers, individuals may find it helpful to engage with practices that enhance intuition and awareness. Meditation, journaling, or creative expression can provide opportunities to explore the symbols that arise and to connect with the deeper messages they convey. These practices offer a space for introspection and integration, allowing the whispers to unfold and reveal their wisdom.

Moreover, sharing experiences and interpretations with others can enrich the process of understanding symbolism in whispers. Engaging in conversations or participating in groups focused on spiritual exploration can provide diverse perspectives and foster a sense of community. Through dialogue and shared reflection, individuals can gain new insights and deepen their connection to the symbolism present in their lives.

Whispering Techniques and Practices

The art of whispering is a delicate and profound practice that bridges the gap between the conscious mind and the subtle energies that surround us. Whispering techniques are not limited to the mere act of speaking softly; they involve a deep attunement to the energies and vibrations within and around us, allowing for communication with the unseen and the divine. Through these techniques, individuals can access intuitive insights, hidden knowledge, and spiritual guidance, enriching their lives with clarity and purpose.

To begin exploring whispering techniques, one must cultivate a state of openness and receptivity. This involves creating a quiet, sacred space where the mind can settle and distractions are minimized. Setting the stage for whispering requires intention and mindfulness, whether through lighting candles, burning incense, or simply finding a tranquil corner in nature. The environment should be one that encourages relaxation and presence, allowing the practitioner to focus inwardly and attune to the subtleties of whispering.

Breathwork is a foundational element in whispering practices, serving as a bridge between the physical and etheric realms. By engaging in conscious breathing, individuals can calm the mind and center the body, creating a harmonious state for whispering. Techniques such as diaphragmatic breathing, where one inhales deeply into the belly and exhales slowly, help to release tension and promote a sense of groundedness. As the breath flows rhythmically, it becomes a conduit for energy, facilitating the flow of whispers and insights.

Visualization is another powerful tool in whispering practices, allowing practitioners to connect with the imagery and symbols that may emerge during the process. By closing the eyes and envisioning a serene landscape or a protective light, individuals can create a mental space where whispers can be received without interference. Visualization serves to anchor the mind, fostering a deeper connection to the intuitive and spiritual dimensions.

The practice of listening is central to whispering techniques, requiring a heightened awareness of both internal and external cues. This involves paying attention not only to the words and sounds that may arise but also to the sensations and emotions that accompany them. Active listening encourages a dialogue with the whispers, where the practitioner remains present and engaged, ready to receive whatever messages may come through. It is important to approach this practice with an open heart and mind, free from judgment or expectation.

Affirmations and mantras can be incorporated into whispering practices to enhance focus and intention. By repeating positive statements or sacred phrases, individuals can align their energy with the desired outcome, amplifying the power of the whispers. These verbal expressions serve as anchors, helping to maintain concentration and reinforce the connection to the spiritual realm. Whether spoken aloud or silently, affirmations and mantras can guide the practitioner into a deeper state of awareness and attunement.

Journaling is an effective technique for capturing and reflecting on the whispers received during practice. By writing down thoughts, impressions, and insights, individuals can document their experiences and track patterns or themes that may emerge over time. Journaling provides a tangible record of the whispering journey, offering opportunities for introspection and growth. It allows practitioners to revisit and reinterpret the messages, gaining new perspectives and understanding.

Incorporating movement into whispering practices can also enhance the flow of energy and facilitate the reception of whispers. Gentle movements, such as yoga or tai chi, help to release physical tension and promote a state of relaxation and openness. By engaging the body in this way, individuals can create a dynamic interplay between movement and stillness, allowing whispers to arise naturally and effortlessly. Movement serves as a form of expression, enabling the practitioner to embody the whispers and integrate them into their being.

Silence, paradoxically, is a crucial component of whispering practices. In silence, the mind can quiet its chatter, creating a space for whispers to be heard. This involves embracing moments of stillness and solitude, where the absence of sound becomes a canvas for the subtle communication of whispers. Silence encourages reflection and introspection, allowing individuals to connect with their inner wisdom and the messages that lie beyond the surface.

For those seeking to deepen their whispering practice, guided meditations and sound therapy can provide valuable support. Guided meditations offer structured journeys into the realm of whispers, using imagery and narration to facilitate exploration and discovery. Sound therapy, through instruments like singing bowls or tuning forks, can enhance the vibrational environment, attuning the practitioner to the frequencies of whispers. These tools serve as aids in the whispering process, offering pathways to deeper connection and understanding.

Community and shared practice can also enrich the whispering experience, providing opportunities for learning and growth. Engaging with like-minded individuals in group settings or workshops can foster a sense of connection and support, as practitioners share their insights and experiences. The collective energy of a group can amplify the power of whispers, creating a synergistic environment for exploration and discovery.

Case Studies of Whisper Phenomena

Whisper phenomena have intrigued and mystified individuals across cultures and centuries, manifesting in various forms and leaving profound impressions on those who experience them. These phenomena often carry messages, insights, or warnings from the unseen realms, inviting deeper contemplation and understanding. By examining case studies of whisper phenomena, we can gain valuable insights into their nature and significance, offering both guidance and inspiration for those seeking to connect with these subtle communications.

One compelling case involves the experiences of a woman named Eleanor, who began noticing faint whispers during her daily meditation practice. Initially dismissing them as mere distractions, she soon realized that these whispers carried specific messages related to her personal struggles and life choices. Over time, Eleanor recorded the whispers in a journal, noting patterns and themes that emerged. One recurring message urged her to reconcile with her estranged brother, a relationship that had been strained for years. Motivated by the whispers, Eleanor reached out to her brother, leading to a heartfelt reunion and healing of past wounds. This case highlights how whispers can serve as catalysts for personal growth and reconciliation, prompting individuals to make meaningful changes in their lives.

In another case, a musician named Carlos experienced whispers while composing music late at night. These whispers seemed to guide his creative process, offering melodic phrases and lyrical ideas that resonated deeply with him. Initially skeptical, Carlos decided to embrace the whispers, allowing them to influence his compositions. The resulting music, infused with the essence of the whispers, resonated with audiences on a profound level, leading to unexpected success and recognition. Carlos's experience illustrates how whispers can serve as sources of inspiration and creativity, guiding individuals toward their true artistic expression.

A third case involves a small community in a remote village, where whispers were heard collectively by several residents during a period of turmoil and uncertainty. These whispers, often perceived during moments of quiet reflection, conveyed messages of unity and resilience. As the community members shared their experiences, they discovered common themes and insights, which encouraged them to come together and address the challenges they faced. This collective experience of whisper phenomena fostered a sense of solidarity and strength, empowering the community to navigate adversity with renewed hope and determination.

Another intriguing case study centers on a young child named Mia, who began mentioning whispers she heard while playing alone in her backyard. Her parents, initially concerned, decided to observe and support Mia's experiences. The whispers, as described by Mia, often conveyed messages of encouragement and guidance, particularly during moments of fear or uncertainty. Recognizing the potential significance of these whispers, Mia's parents encouraged her to express her thoughts and feelings through art and storytelling. This creative outlet allowed Mia to process and integrate the whispers, fostering her emotional and spiritual development. Mia's case underscores the importance of nurturing and supporting children's experiences with whisper phenomena, allowing them to explore and understand these subtle communications in a safe and creative environment.

In a more dramatic case, a man named David experienced whispers during a near-death experience following a serious accident. As he hovered between life and death, David heard whispers that conveyed messages of love, forgiveness, and the interconnectedness of all beings. These whispers left an indelible impression on David, profoundly altering his perspective on life and death. Upon recovering, David dedicated his life to sharing the messages he received, becoming an advocate for compassion and spiritual awareness. His case demonstrates how whispers can emerge during transformative experiences, offering insights that lead to profound shifts in consciousness and purpose.

An additional case involves a group of hikers who encountered whispers while exploring an ancient forest. These whispers, perceived as gentle murmurs carried by the wind, seemed to convey the history and wisdom of the land. Intrigued, the hikers took time to listen and reflect, gaining a deeper appreciation for the natural world and their place within it. This experience inspired them to become advocates for environmental conservation, driven by the understanding that whispers can connect individuals to the earth and its timeless wisdom. The hikers' case highlights the potential for whispers to foster a deeper connection with nature and inspire actions that honor and protect the environment.

These case studies of whisper phenomena reveal the diverse ways in which whispers can manifest and impact individuals and communities. Whether serving as guides for personal transformation, sources of creative inspiration, catalysts for healing and reconciliation, or connectors to the natural world, whispers offer valuable insights and opportunities for growth. By examining these cases, we gain a richer understanding of the potential and significance of whisper phenomena, encouraging us to remain open to the subtle messages that may shape our lives.

The diversity of experiences shared in these case studies also emphasizes the importance of context and individual interpretation. While the whispers may carry universal themes, their specific meanings and implications are often deeply personal, resonating uniquely with each individual or group. This underscores the value of personal reflection and exploration in understanding and integrating whisper phenomena into one's life.

For those seeking to engage with whisper phenomena, these case studies offer both inspiration and practical insights. They encourage individuals to cultivate openness and receptivity, to trust their intuition, and to embrace the whispers that emerge in their lives. By doing so, individuals can access the wisdom and guidance that whispers offer, navigating their paths with greater clarity, purpose, and connection to the unseen realms.

The Influence of Whispers on Human Behavior

Whispers, those subtle, often imperceptible voices that linger at the edge of consciousness, hold a remarkable sway over human behavior. They navigate the liminal spaces between thought and action, influencing decisions, emotions, and interactions in ways that can be both profound and enigmatic.

Whether arising from the depths of one's own psyche or perceived as messages from the spiritual realm, whispers can guide, caution, or inspire individuals, shaping their paths in unexpected ways.

The influence of whispers on decision-making is a fascinating aspect of human behavior. Individuals often experience a sense of inner knowing or intuition, a whisper that nudges them toward a particular choice or direction. This intuitive guidance can manifest as a gut feeling, an inexplicable certainty that defies logical analysis. Such whispers encourage individuals to trust their instincts, often leading them to make decisions that align with their true desires and values, even when external circumstances suggest otherwise. By listening to these whispers, individuals can navigate complex situations with confidence and clarity, trusting in the wisdom that emerges from within.

Emotional responses are another domain where whispers exert significant influence. Whispers can serve as mirrors, reflecting back the emotions that lie beneath the surface of consciousness. They may amplify feelings of joy, sorrow, or fear, drawing attention to the emotional landscape and prompting individuals to explore and understand their inner worlds. In this way, whispers can act as catalysts for emotional growth and healing, encouraging individuals to confront and process unresolved feelings. By acknowledging and engaging with the whispers of emotion, individuals can cultivate greater self-awareness and emotional resilience, fostering a deeper connection to themselves and others.

Whispers also play a role in shaping interpersonal relationships, subtly guiding the dynamics of communication and connection. In moments of tension or conflict, a whisper may arise, urging compassion, empathy, or understanding. These whispers can influence how individuals approach and resolve disagreements, encouraging them to listen actively and respond with kindness. Similarly, whispers of intuition may guide individuals toward forming meaningful connections, drawing them to kindred spirits or potential collaborators. By heeding these whispers, individuals can build relationships that are authentic and nourishing, grounded in mutual respect and shared purpose.

Creativity and artistic expression are realms where whispers often flourish, inspiring individuals to explore new ideas and perspectives. Whispers of inspiration can ignite the creative spark, offering glimpses of possibility that transcend the limitations of conventional thought. Artists, writers, and musicians frequently describe the sensation of being guided by whispers, as if a muse were whispering ideas and visions into their minds. These creative whispers encourage individuals to take risks, to experiment with form and content, and to push the boundaries of their craft. By embracing the whispers of creativity, individuals can access a wellspring of innovation and originality, contributing to the richness of human culture and expression.

In the context of personal growth and self-discovery, whispers serve as gentle guides, illuminating the path toward greater understanding and fulfillment. They may reveal hidden talents, unacknowledged desires, or uncharted aspects of the self, inviting individuals to explore and embrace their full potential. Whispers can prompt moments of introspection, encouraging individuals to examine their beliefs, motivations, and aspirations. By engaging with these whispers, individuals can embark on a journey of self-exploration and transformation, uncovering the layers of their identity and aligning their lives with their deepest truths.

The influence of whispers on human behavior extends beyond the individual, affecting collective consciousness and societal dynamics. Whispers can inspire movements for change, calling attention to injustices or inequities that demand action. Throughout history, whispers have played a role in igniting social and cultural revolutions, as individuals listen to the murmurs of conscience and respond with courage and conviction. These collective whispers encourage communities to come together, to envision and create a more just and compassionate world.

In understanding the influence of whispers on human behavior, it is essential to recognize the interplay between the conscious and subconscious mind. Whispers often originate from the subconscious, where memories, emotions, and archetypal symbols reside. They act as bridges between these inner realms and the conscious mind, offering insights and guidance that may not be readily accessible through rational thought alone. By cultivating a practice of mindfulness and reflection, individuals can enhance their receptivity to whispers, allowing them to emerge and inform their actions with greater clarity and purpose.

To harness the influence of whispers, individuals can engage in practices that promote attunement and awareness. Meditation, journaling, and creative expression are valuable tools for connecting with the whispers that reside within. These practices create space for whispers to surface, offering opportunities for exploration and integration. By dedicating time to these practices, individuals can develop a deeper relationship with the whispers, enhancing their ability to listen and respond with intention.

The influence of whispers on human behavior is a testament to the complexity and richness of the human experience. They remind us of the interconnectedness of mind, body, and spirit, and the ways in which subtle energies and insights can shape our lives. By embracing the whispers and the guidance they offer, individuals can navigate their journeys with greater awareness and authenticity, honoring the whispers that call them to grow, transform, and connect with the world around them.

Whisper Networks and Their Impact

Whisper networks, those informal channels of communication that exist beneath the surface of formal interactions, wield a quiet yet formidable influence in various social and professional settings. These networks, often composed of individuals who share common experiences, values, or goals, serve as conduits for sharing information, insights, and support. They operate on trust and confidentiality, allowing members to exchange crucial knowledge that may not be accessible through official channels. The impact of whisper networks can be significant, shaping decisions, fostering solidarity, and driving change.

The origins of whisper networks can be traced to the need for safe spaces where individuals can speak freely and candidly without fear of judgment or repercussions. In professional environments, these networks often emerge among colleagues who seek to navigate the complexities of workplace dynamics, offering advice on matters such as career advancement, handling difficult situations, or understanding unwritten rules. By providing a platform for open dialogue, whisper networks empower individuals to make informed decisions and advocate for their interests.

One of the primary impacts of whisper networks is their ability to facilitate the sharing of critical information. In many organizations, official communication channels may be limited or restricted by hierarchies, leaving gaps in the flow of information. Whisper networks fill these gaps by disseminating insights that are essential for understanding the broader context of a situation. For example, in a corporate setting, a whisper network might alert employees to impending organizational changes, allowing them to prepare accordingly. This access to information can lead to more strategic decision-making, as individuals are better equipped to anticipate and respond to developments.

Whisper networks also play a crucial role in fostering a sense of community and belonging, particularly for individuals who may feel marginalized or isolated within their environments. By connecting like-minded individuals, these networks create a support system that encourages collaboration and mutual aid. Members of whisper networks often share common challenges or experiences, such as navigating gender or racial biases, and can offer each other guidance and encouragement. This sense of solidarity can be empowering, reinforcing the idea that individuals are not alone in their struggles and that collective action can lead to meaningful change.

In addition to providing support and information, whisper networks can serve as catalysts for advocacy and social change. When individuals come together to share their experiences and insights, they can identify patterns of behavior or systemic issues that require attention. Whisper networks have been instrumental in movements that challenge injustices and advocate for equity, as they enable individuals to organize and amplify their voices. By leveraging the power of collective knowledge and action, whisper networks have the potential to influence policies, shift cultural norms, and drive progress.

Despite their positive impact, whisper networks are not without challenges. Maintaining confidentiality and trust is paramount, as breaches can undermine the integrity of the network and compromise the safety of its members. Additionally, the informal nature of whisper networks can sometimes lead to the spread of misinformation or rumors, which can have unintended consequences. It is essential for members to approach information critically and verify its accuracy before acting upon it.

To maximize the benefits of whisper networks, individuals can take proactive steps to nurture and sustain these connections. Building a whisper network requires cultivating relationships based on trust and mutual respect. This involves active listening, empathetic communication, and a willingness to share one's own insights and experiences. By fostering an environment where members feel valued and heard, whisper networks can thrive and continue to provide support and guidance.

Moreover, individuals can leverage technology to enhance the reach and effectiveness of whisper networks. Online platforms and social media can facilitate communication and collaboration, allowing members to connect across geographical boundaries. However, it is important to balance the convenience of digital communication with the need for privacy and security. Establishing clear guidelines for online interactions can help protect the integrity of the network and maintain confidentiality.

Organizations can also play a role in supporting whisper networks by creating inclusive environments that encourage open dialogue and collaboration. By recognizing the value of informal communication channels, organizations can foster a culture of transparency and trust, where employees feel empowered to share their insights and contribute to the collective knowledge. This can lead to more innovative and effective solutions, as diverse perspectives are brought to the forefront.

In the broader societal context, whisper networks contribute to the democratization of information, challenging traditional power structures and enabling individuals to assert their agency. They offer a means of resistance against oppressive systems, providing a platform for marginalized voices to be heard and for grassroots movements to gain momentum. By amplifying the voices of those who have been historically silenced, whisper networks can drive social change and promote justice and equity.

Chapter 5: Haunting Echoes of the Past

Echoes in Ancient History

Throughout the annals of ancient history, whispers have echoed with profound significance, weaving themselves into the fabric of human civilization. These echoes can be found in myths, legends, and historical accounts, serving as conduits of knowledge, wisdom, and divine communication. The ancients understood whispers not merely as auditory phenomena but as messages from the beyond—clues that guided actions, shaped beliefs, and influenced the destiny of entire cultures.

Consider the ancient Greek oracle of Delphi, a quintessential embodiment of whispers in history. Perched atop Mount Parnassus, the oracle served as a sacred intermediary between the gods and mortals. Pilgrims traveled from distant lands to seek the oracle's cryptic whispers, delivered through the priestess known as the Pythia. Her utterances, often veiled in ambiguity, were believed to be the voice of Apollo himself, providing guidance on matters ranging from personal dilemmas to affairs of state. These whispers, enigmatic yet revered, held the power to alter the course of events, as individuals and leaders interpreted and acted upon them with faith in their divine origins.

In ancient Egypt, whispers took on a spiritual dimension within the context of religious rituals and funerary practices. The Egyptians believed in the existence of the ka, a spiritual double that accompanied each person through life and into the afterlife. Whispers were thought to be the communication of the ka, guiding the living and the deceased through the complexities of existence. Priests and priestesses, adept in the art of listening to these spiritual whispers, conducted ceremonies and rites to ensure the harmonious journey of the soul. The hieroglyphs etched on temple walls and sarcophagi stand as silent testimonies to the whispers that shaped the Egyptian understanding of life, death, and eternity.

The ancient Chinese, too, held a profound appreciation for whispers, particularly in the realm of philosophy and governance. The Daoist tradition, with its emphasis on harmony with the natural world, regarded whispers as expressions of the Dao—the underlying force that governs the universe. Laozi's "Tao Te Ching" is replete with references to the subtle whispers of nature, urging adherents to attune themselves to the quiet wisdom of the world around them. In governance, Confucian scholars listened for the whispers of the people, advocating for a ruler's moral duty to heed the needs and concerns of their subjects. These whispers informed the ethical and political frameworks that guided Chinese civilization for millennia.

The echoes of whispers can also be traced to the ancient Celtic druids, who revered the natural world as a source of sacred knowledge. The druids, as spiritual leaders and keepers of wisdom, were believed to communicate with the spirits of the land through whispers carried on the wind. These whispers, interpreted through rituals and divination, offered guidance on matters of community welfare and spiritual balance. The druids' deep connection to the earth and its whispers underscored their role as mediators between the human and the divine, fostering a harmonious relationship with the environment.

In the rich tapestry of Hindu mythology, whispers often manifest as divine revelations received by sages and seers during meditation. The Vedas, ancient sacred texts of India, are said to have been transmitted through whispers from the cosmos to enlightened sages. These whispers, captured in hymns and verses, contain profound spiritual truths and rituals that continue to guide Hindu practice and belief. The idea of whispers as a means of divine revelation underscores the importance of introspection and spiritual attunement in accessing higher knowledge.

The biblical tradition is replete with instances of whispers that conveyed divine will and guidance. Prophets, such as Elijah and Samuel, are depicted as receiving whispers from God, instructing them on their missions and responsibilities. These whispered communications often occurred in moments of solitude and reflection, emphasizing the need for silence and receptivity in discerning the divine message. The biblical narratives highlight the transformative power of whispers, as they catalyzed pivotal events in the history of the Israelites and their relationship with the divine.

In Mesoamerican cultures, whispers were integral to the practice of shamanism and the interpretation of omens. Shamans, as conduits between the physical and spiritual worlds, listened to the whispers of the ancestors and spirits, seeking guidance on healing, agriculture, and communal matters. These whispers, whether perceived during trance states or through natural phenomena, informed the shamanic practices that sustained the cultural and spiritual life of Mesoamerican societies. The reverence for whispers as messengers of the unseen world underscored the interconnectedness of all existence in these cultures.

As we traverse the echoes of whispers in ancient history, we witness their enduring impact on human thought and civilization. Whispers served as bridges between the known and the unknown, guiding individuals and societies in their quest for understanding and meaning. They remind us of the timeless nature of communication beyond words, inviting us to listen with open hearts and minds to the wisdom that transcends the ages.

The Power of Echoes in Storytelling

Echoes in storytelling possess a remarkable power, resonating across generations and cultures with their ability to captivate, instruct, and inspire. They are the reverberations of themes, motifs, and archetypes that transcend time and place, weaving a tapestry of collective human experience. These echoes are not mere repetitions; they are the threads that connect diverse narratives, imbuing stories with depth and resonance. Understanding the power of these echoes enriches our appreciation of storytelling and enhances our ability to engage audiences through shared cultural and emotional touchstones.

The concept of echoes in storytelling can be traced back to the oral traditions of ancient civilizations, where stories were passed down through generations, each retelling adding layers of meaning and nuance. The repetition of key elements within these stories served as a mnemonic device, aiding in their preservation and transmission. More importantly, these echoes allowed listeners to draw connections between the stories and their own lives, fostering a sense of belonging and continuity. By echoing familiar themes and archetypes, storytellers ensured that their narratives remained relevant and relatable, regardless of the passage of time.

One of the most potent echoes in storytelling is the hero's journey, an archetypal narrative structure identified by mythologist Joseph Campbell. This structure, which appears in countless stories across cultures, follows a protagonist's departure from the ordinary world, their initiation into a realm of adventure and trials, and their eventual return home transformed. The hero's journey resonates because it echoes the universal human experience of growth and transformation, inviting audiences to see themselves in the hero's struggles and triumphs. By tapping into this deep-seated archetype, storytellers can engage audiences on both an intellectual and emotional level, creating narratives that resonate with authenticity and power.

Another powerful echo in storytelling is the theme of love and sacrifice. This theme pervades literature, film, and folklore, manifesting in myriad forms—from the selfless love of a parent for a child to the romantic sacrifices made in the name of love. These stories echo our deepest desires and fears, exploring the complexities of human relationships and the lengths to which individuals will go for those they care about. By incorporating this timeless theme, storytellers can evoke powerful emotions and create connections with audiences, highlighting the shared humanity that underlies diverse cultural expressions.

The use of echoes in storytelling also extends to the incorporation of symbols and motifs that carry cultural and historical significance. These symbols, whether they be the apple in "Snow White," the ring in "The Lord of the Rings," or the labyrinth in Greek mythology, serve as anchors for meaning and interpretation. They evoke a sense of familiarity and continuity, drawing on collective memories and associations to enrich the narrative. By echoing these symbols, storytellers can layer their stories with meaning, inviting audiences to engage in a deeper exploration of the themes and messages conveyed.

In addition to thematic and symbolic echoes, storytelling is enriched by echoes of style and form. The use of certain narrative techniques, such as foreshadowing, parallel storylines, or nonlinear timelines, can create echoes within a story that heighten tension and intrigue. These structural echoes invite audiences to piece together the narrative puzzle, enhancing their engagement and investment in the story. By skillfully weaving these echoes into their narratives, storytellers can create a sense of coherence and unity, guiding audiences through a satisfying and immersive storytelling experience.

The power of echoes in storytelling is also evident in the realm of adaptation and reinterpretation. By reimagining classic tales through new lenses, storytellers can create narratives that resonate with contemporary audiences while honoring the essence of the original stories. These echoes of familiar tales invite audiences to consider timeless themes in new contexts, fostering reflection and dialogue about the evolving nature of human experience. Whether through modern retellings of Shakespearean plays or cinematic adaptations of ancient myths, these echoes serve as bridges between past and present, enriching the cultural tapestry with their enduring relevance.

For storytellers seeking to harness the power of echoes, it is essential to cultivate an awareness of the cultural and emotional resonances that underpin their narratives. This involves a deep engagement with the stories, symbols, and archetypes that have shaped human consciousness, as well as a sensitivity to the diverse experiences and perspectives of their audiences. By weaving these echoes into their storytelling, creators can craft narratives that resonate across boundaries, inviting audiences to embark on journeys of discovery and transformation.

Moreover, storytellers can experiment with echoes to create innovative and dynamic narratives that challenge conventions and expand the possibilities of storytelling. By playing with familiar elements and subverting expectations, they can create stories that surprise and captivate audiences, while still drawing on the echoes that ground their narratives in shared experience. This balance of familiarity and novelty is key to crafting stories that are both engaging and meaningful, offering audiences new insights into the timeless themes that echo through our lives.

The Science Behind Echoes

The phenomenon of echoes is a captivating intersection of physics and perception, offering insights into the nature of sound and its reverberations through space. At its core, an echo is the reflection of sound waves off a surface, returning to the listener's ear after a brief delay. This seemingly simple occurrence is governed by complex principles that bridge the realms of acoustics and human experience, revealing the intricate dynamics that underpin our auditory world.

Sound, as understood in scientific terms, is a mechanical wave that propagates through a medium such as air, water, or solid materials. When a sound wave encounters an obstacle or surface, a portion of its energy is absorbed, while the rest is reflected back. The time delay between the original sound and its echo is determined by the distance between the source and the reflecting surface, as well as the speed of sound in the medium. In air, sound travels at approximately 343 meters per second, although this speed can vary with changes in temperature, humidity, and atmospheric pressure.

The perceptible delay that characterizes an echo typically occurs when the reflecting surface is more than 17 meters away from the listener. This distance allows for a time gap of approximately 0.1 seconds between the original sound and its reflection, which the human ear can distinguish as a separate auditory event. In environments where the reflecting surface is closer, the reflected sound merges with the original, enhancing its amplitude and creating the auditory phenomenon known as reverberation. Reverberation contributes to the richness of sound in enclosed spaces, such as concert halls and cathedrals, where multiple reflections overlap to create a sustained and harmonious auditory experience.

The study of echoes extends beyond the basic principles of reflection and delay, encompassing the ways in which different surfaces and materials influence the behavior of sound. Smooth, hard surfaces, such as stone or metal, are highly reflective and produce clear echoes, while soft, porous materials, like carpets or curtains, absorb sound and diminish echo strength. The angle at which sound waves strike a surface also plays a crucial role; oblique angles can cause sound to scatter, while perpendicular angles often result in a more direct reflection.

In natural environments, echoes can provide valuable information about the surrounding landscape. The phenomenon of echolocation, employed by species such as bats and dolphins, demonstrates the practical applications of echoes in navigation and hunting. These animals emit high-frequency sounds and interpret the returning echoes to determine the distance, size, and shape of objects in their vicinity.

This sophisticated biological sonar system allows them to navigate complex environments and locate prey with remarkable precision, showcasing the adaptive power of echoes in the natural world.

For humans, echoes have found diverse applications in technology and industry, from architectural acoustics to medical imaging. In architecture, understanding the behavior of echoes is essential for designing spaces with optimal sound qualities. Architects and acousticians collaborate to manipulate the reflective properties of surfaces, ensuring that sound is evenly distributed and that echoes do not interfere with clarity. This is particularly important in venues such as theaters and recording studios, where sound quality is paramount.

In the realm of medical imaging, echoes form the basis of ultrasound technology, a non-invasive diagnostic tool that uses high-frequency sound waves to create images of internal body structures. During an ultrasound examination, sound waves are transmitted into the body and reflect off tissues and organs. The returning echoes are captured and converted into visual images, allowing healthcare professionals to assess conditions and monitor fetal development with accuracy and safety.

The scientific exploration of echoes also extends to the field of seismology, where the study of seismic echoes helps researchers understand the Earth's internal structure. When seismic waves generated by earthquakes or artificial explosions travel through the Earth, they reflect and refract at the boundaries between different layers of rock. By analyzing these echoes, seismologists can infer the composition and properties of the Earth's interior, contributing to our knowledge of geological processes and the dynamics of tectonic plates.

Echoes have also played a pivotal role in the development of radar and sonar technologies, which utilize the principles of sound and electromagnetic wave reflection to detect and locate objects. Radar, which operates in the radio wave spectrum, is widely used in aviation, meteorology, and military applications to track aircraft, monitor weather patterns, and detect incoming threats. Sonar, on the other hand, uses sound waves to map underwater environments and locate submarines, shipwrecks, and marine life. Both technologies rely on the analysis of echoes to provide critical information about the position and movement of objects.

Beyond their scientific applications, echoes have captured the human imagination, inspiring artistic and philosophical reflections on the nature of sound and memory. In literature and music, echoes are often used as metaphors for the persistence of ideas, emotions, and experiences, suggesting a resonance that transcends time and space. The repetition and reflection inherent in echoes evoke a sense of continuity and connection, inviting contemplation of the ways in which the past informs the present and future.

Echoes in Haunted Locations

The phenomenon of echoes in haunted locations is a compelling interplay between acoustics, human psychology, and cultural narratives. These echoes, both literal and metaphorical, contribute significantly to the eerie atmosphere of haunted sites, enhancing their reputation as repositories of the supernatural. Understanding the role of echoes in these settings requires an exploration of how sound, environment, and perception intertwine to create experiences that captivate and unsettle the human psyche.

In haunted locations, echoes often manifest as disembodied voices, footsteps, or unexplained noises that seem to originate from nowhere. These auditory phenomena can be attributed to the unique acoustic properties of the environment. The architecture of old buildings, with their long corridors, high ceilings, and hard surfaces, can create conditions that amplify and distort sound. Even the faintest noise, such as a creaking floorboard or a distant whisper, can reverberate and transform into something more sinister. This acoustic effect, combined with the heightened emotional state of individuals in such settings, can lead to the perception of ghostly presences.

The psychological aspect of echoes in haunted locations cannot be underestimated. Human perception is inherently influenced by expectations and beliefs, and the power of suggestion plays a crucial role in shaping experiences of the paranormal. When individuals enter a site reputed to be haunted, they often expect to encounter something unusual or otherworldly. This anticipation can prime the mind to interpret ordinary sounds as paranormal, transforming mundane echoes into evidence of supernatural activity. The brain's tendency to seek patterns and meaning further contributes to this phenomenon, as it attempts to make sense of ambiguous auditory stimuli.

Cultural narratives and folklore surrounding haunted locations also enhance the perception of echoes as harbingers of the spectral. Stories of tragic events, restless spirits, and unfinished business imbue these sites with a sense of mystery and dread. These tales, passed down through generations, create a collective memory that influences individual experiences. When echoes occur in such contexts, they are often interpreted through the lens of these narratives, reinforcing the belief in the presence of ghosts. The interplay between sound and story creates a feedback loop, where echoes amplify the lore, and the lore, in turn, colors the perception of echoes.

Certain locations are particularly renowned for their haunted echoes, drawing visitors eager to experience their spine-chilling acoustics. The Winchester Mystery House in California, with its labyrinthine architecture, is one such site. Built by Sarah Winchester, heiress to the Winchester rifle fortune, the house is said to be haunted by the spirits of those killed by the rifles. The unconventional design, featuring staircases leading nowhere and hidden rooms, creates a complex soundscape that enhances the perception of ghostly activity. Visitors often report hearing inexplicable footsteps, whispers, and other unsettling noises that seem to emanate from the shadows.

Similarly, the ancient castles of Europe are steeped in tales of hauntings, where echoes play a central role in the spectral encounters of visitors. The stone walls and cavernous halls of these fortresses create ideal conditions for sound to linger and transform. In places like Edinburgh Castle, where the history is rich with conflict and intrigue, echoes of the past are said to manifest as ghostly apparitions and mysterious sounds. The interplay of history, architecture, and acoustics fosters an environment ripe for paranormal interpretation, captivating those who walk its storied corridors.

In addition to architectural elements, natural settings can also contribute to the phenomenon of echoes in haunted locations. Forests, caves, and cliffs, with their natural acoustic properties, can create eerie soundscapes that inspire tales of hauntings. The dense foliage of a forest, for example, can muffle and distort sound, creating the illusion of whispers carried on the wind. Caves, with their echoing chambers, amplify the smallest noises, transforming them into ghostly sounds that seem to emanate from the depths of the earth. These natural echoes, when combined with the primal fear of the unknown, contribute to the aura of mystery and unease that surrounds such locations.

The role of technology in capturing and analyzing echoes in haunted locations has also become an integral part of modern paranormal investigations. Devices such as digital recorders, electromagnetic field meters, and thermal cameras are employed to detect and document unexplained phenomena. In particular, electronic voice phenomena (EVP) recordings, which capture sounds not heard at the time of recording, have become a staple of ghost hunting. These recordings often reveal faint echoes and whispers, interpreted as communications from the spirit world. While skeptics attribute such phenomena to auditory pareidolia or equipment artifacts, believers see them as compelling evidence of the supernatural.

Despite the skepticism surrounding haunted echoes, their cultural and psychological impact remains profound. They invite us to explore the boundaries between reality and imagination, challenging our understanding of perception and belief. Whether one views them as manifestations of the supernatural or as products of acoustic and psychological processes, echoes in haunted locations continue to captivate our collective imagination.

For those intrigued by the intersection of sound, space, and the spectral, exploring haunted locations offers a unique opportunity to engage with the mysteries of the unknown. By approaching these sites with an open mind and a critical ear, one can appreciate the complex interplay of factors that contribute to the haunted experience. Whether it's the creaking of ancient floorboards, the whisper of a breeze through a drafty hall, or the echo of footsteps in an empty room, these sounds remind us of the enduring power of echoes to evoke wonder and curiosity.

Personal Echo Experiences

Personal experiences with echoes are often deeply profound, offering insight into both the external environment and the inner workings of the human mind. These experiences can range from the mundane to the mystical, each echo carrying with it a story that reflects the unique interplay of sound, memory, and emotion. The significance of personal echo experiences lies in their ability to connect individuals to specific moments in time, evoking memories and emotions that transcend the immediate auditory event.

Consider the experience of standing in a vast canyon, where the sound of your voice reverberates off the ancient rock walls. The echo returns, altered by its journey, carrying with it a sense of awe and insignificance in the face of nature's grandeur. This interaction with the landscape not only highlights the acoustic properties of the environment but also serves as a reminder of one's place within the larger tapestry of the natural world. Such experiences often leave a lasting impression, imprinting themselves in memory and becoming a touchstone for reflection and contemplation.

Similarly, echoes encountered in urban environments can evoke a spectrum of emotions, from nostalgia to curiosity. Imagine walking through a bustling city street, where the chatter of passersby, the honking of horns, and the distant hum of construction blend into a symphony of urban life. In the midst of this cacophony, a sudden echo—a shout, a laugh, a snippet of conversation—can capture attention and resonate in unexpected ways. These fleeting moments of auditory reflection can transport us back to childhood memories of playing in a city park or evoke a sense of connection to the vibrant pulse of urban existence.

Personal echo experiences are not limited to the natural or urban landscapes; they can also occur within the confines of our homes. The familiar echo of footsteps in a hallway, the resonant clang of a pot in the kitchen, or the soft murmur of a voice in a neighboring room can create a comforting or unsettling atmosphere. These domestic echoes often carry an emotional weight, colored by the relationships and memories associated with the space. A creaking floorboard might bring to mind a cherished family member, while the echo of a distant television program might evoke a sense of solitude or longing.

In addition to their sensory and emotional dimensions, personal echo experiences can serve as catalysts for creativity and introspection. Writers, musicians, and artists often draw inspiration from the echoes that permeate their surroundings, using them as metaphors for the themes and emotions they wish to explore. The act of listening to and interpreting echoes can lead to moments of insight and inspiration, sparking new ideas and perspectives. For many, the process of engaging with echoes becomes a form of meditation, inviting a deeper awareness of the present moment and the myriad connections between sound, space, and self.

The psychological impact of echoes on personal experience is further influenced by individual differences in perception and interpretation. Some people may possess heightened sensitivity to sound, making them more attuned to the nuances of echoes in their environment. Others may have specific associations or memories linked to particular sounds, shaping their emotional response to echoes. The subjective nature of these experiences underscores the importance of personal context in understanding and appreciating the richness of echoes in everyday life.

For those interested in cultivating a deeper awareness of personal echo experiences, several practices can enhance one's ability to listen and connect with their auditory environment. Mindful listening, for example, involves paying close attention to the sounds around us, without judgment or distraction. By focusing on the subtleties of sound and the way it interacts with space, individuals can develop a greater appreciation for the complexity and beauty of their auditory world. This practice can be particularly rewarding in natural settings, where the echoes of birdsong, rustling leaves, and flowing water create a symphony of sound that invites contemplation and wonder.